My Broken Pieces— His Yielded Clay

EVIE G.

ISBN 978-1-63874-083-4 (paperback)
ISBN 978-1-63874-158-9 (hardcover)
ISBN 978-1-63874-084-1 (digital)

Copyright © 2021 by Evie G.

All rights reserved. No part of this publication may be reproduced, distributed, or transmitted in any form or by any means, including photocopying, recording, or other electronic or mechanical methods without the prior written permission of the publisher. For permission requests, solicit the publisher via the address below.

Christian Faith Publishing, Inc.
832 Park Avenue
Meadville, PA 16335
www.christianfaithpublishing.com

Printed in the United States of America

CONTENTS

Introduction 5
Chapter 1:   Dear God, Are You Sure about This? 7
Chapter 2:   God Specializes in Metamorphosis 10
Chapter 3:   That No Good, Cotton-Pickin' Summer 13
Chapter 4:   The Lies of Satan Are Alive and Well 20
Chapter 5:   We Learned to Walk on Eggshells 23
Chapter 6:   My Divine Appointment with Forgiveness 25
Chapter 7:   If Not for God's Grace
             and a Praying Grandmother 29
Chapter 8:   There's Got to Be a Better Way! 33
Chapter 9:   The Day of Imploding Reckoning 36
Chapter 10: The Beauty of Forgiveness 40
Chapter 11: The Journey Navigated by the Master's Hand 42
Chapter 12: The Devil Dancing on My Grave 45
Chapter 13: God, if You Exist, Where Are You? 51
Chapter 14: Meeting the Savior of My Soul 54
Chapter 15: God—the Way Maker, the Healer, and
             Chain Breaker! 57
Chapter 16: Our Charlie Brown Christmas 63
Chapter 17: Change My Heart, O God… Make It Ever New 65
Chapter 18: God Never Wastes a Hurt 69
Chapter 19: Visions I Will Never Forget 71

Chapter 20: What's the "Matter" All About?...............................76
Chapter 21: He Will Give You the Desires of Your Heart............80
Chapter 22: God Heard Me the First Time.................................84
Chapter 23: Bang! Went the Little Spinning Gray Cells
  in My Head..87
Chapter 24: God Turns Weeping into Joy in the Morning...........91
Chapter 25: Dear Lord, I Need An MRI!.....................................94
Chapter 26: Worship the Lord Your God,
  and Serve Him Only..99

INTRODUCTION

As far back as I can remember, my voice was silenced as a child. I was not allowed to express myself without fear of doing so. I lived in a climate of anger and hate and was surrounded by a culture of fear. Writing became my intimate place of refuge and release. There I could let go, say it all, and tell my journal what I couldn't say out loud. I had no idea that even then, God was writing my story on the pages of my heart.

So much of my writings were done with tears for ink. But over time, the Lord gave me beauty for ashes and joy for words.

All the events, all the things that happened to me throughout my life kept adding to the pages that would one day become a book—this book. My soul overflows with gratitude for it all.

God had a plan for my life, and it was one that would be seasoned, sprinkled, and sometimes flooded with overwhelming obstacles. In the midst of the chaos and through it all, however, He would bring me to a resting place of solace and peace.

Through the tempests, God would give me two precious, beautiful children who were truly my gifts from the Lord. They were, and are today, the joy and loves of my life. We've been through much heartache together, and they have been, to this day, my loving rocks of Gibraltar. Because of them, I now have the unspeakable blessings of grandchildren and great-grandchildren. I thank God for the love of my family and a new life surrounded by cherished moments with them.

I dedicate this book to God, my Savior and King. He is the real author. My heart's desire is that all who read the following pages will be uplifted with hope and encouragement in what the Lord has done for me. What He's done for me, He can do for you, and *that* you can trust in.

CHAPTER 1

Dear God, Are You Sure about This?

God surely has a sense of humor. The day He created me, the thought of breathing life into me must have made Him smile and chuckle a bit, knowing full well who and what He was fashioning. Deep within me, however, I feel there must also have been a tear welling up inside Him. He knew what He had planned for me and what He would allow to happen in my life. God's plans are always for good, even when it hurts. He never wastes a hurt, never wastes a painful lesson in our lives. In the unfolding of my future, I would discover a scripture in Romans 8:28, "And I know that God works all things together for the good of those who love Him and are called according to His purpose."

I was going to break His heart. Yet by His grace, my life would also bring Him unbridled joy and sighs of laughter.

Ultimately, in my darkest moments of despair, He knew I would seek Him and surrender my life to Him. I imagine He just shook His head, smiled that knowing smile, took a deep breath, and spoke the roller-coaster ride of my life into being.

These are the series of events that delve into the mountaintop and deep valley experiences of my life. I embark on this journey with fear and trembling, being ever so cognizant of the utmost need to stay aligned with God's will in this endeavor.

A little seed, a little storm, and a raging furnace would follow. I've heard it said that it's in the valleys where the richest soil is found.

It flows down from the mountaintops and deposits all its fertile richness in the valleys below. Those valleys are pregnant with nutrients that contribute to healthy, strong growth. Although the mountaintops are beautiful places to be, one can't stay up there for long. The air is too thin, and living things do not flourish there. Such is life. It's down in those valleys where we grow and become stronger. That's where our root grows deep, and we establish a firm foundation. That's where God grows the taproot in our lives, which anchors our soul.

The storms of life come against us. The torrents of rain fall upon us. But our heavenly Father gives us roots that dig deep by the power of His Word. We weather adversities. We learn not only how to overcome the tempests of life but also how to emerge victorious through them. We are like a seed planted that grows and eventually blooms into the creation of God's design.

In time I would find more truth in that than I could ever have imagined.

The refining and purification of gold is done through a crucible type process requiring extreme heat. The fiery furnace serves to separate the dross of impurities until what remains is an element of pure gold.

The dictionary defines a crucible as "a situation of severe trial or in which elements interact, leading to the creation of something new or a very significant and difficult trial or test, experience, or situation."

The crucible always involves a fiery furnace.

In retrospect, that is what I can relate to in the crucible of life that God refined and continues to refine me through. My life was full of the impurities of sin. It took a fiery furnace of severe trials and testing, different life elements interacting, experiences and situations to bring me to a place of surrendering the dross in my life to the refining hand of God.

He would one day take me to His Word, place a mirror in front of me, and reveal Psalm 139:23–24 (AMP): "Search me [thoroughly], O God, and know my heart; test me and know my anxious thoughts. And see if there is any wicked or hurtful way in me and lead me in the everlasting way." And then another is Psalm 51:10

(AMP): "Create in me a clean heart, O God, and renew a right and steadfast spirit within me."

His crucible would indeed create something new in me.

This is an account of God defining for me who I am in His sight. It's about my near-death experience and of the raging anger and hate that spun the downward spiral of my despair, the ones meant by the enemy to destroy me.

I would run the gamut of wrong choices, promiscuity, and hidden, shameful acts growing up. Pain and confusion do that. Satan knew it, and he would lead me down a path of personal regrets to a pit of despair. But *God* knew it as well, and He would lead me upward and heaven bound!

I want to be transparent about the strongholds in my life—all the gods I worshipped and lived for. It's my testimony of shame, bitterness, cancer of the heart, and seeking revenge. But more than that, it's a witness to God's mercy, redemption, and saving grace.

It's HIStory, in the making of MYstory.

CHAPTER 2

God Specializes in Metamorphosis

The dictionary defines one meaning of metamorphosis as "a change of the form or nature of a thing or a person into a completely different one by natural or supernatural means."

I wouldn't change my life experiences even if I could. All the couldas, shouldas, wouldas are mute issues with me. But in God's greater scheme of things, His metamorphosis of the ugly, tragic events of my life served to bring me to a realization that He had His hand on me through it all, even when I didn't feel His presence. You see, He had planned it all even before He took that deep breath and breathed life into me.

He knew I would try everything that the world had to offer before I turned to Him for all the right choices, the right answers. He knew that after seeking all the wrong things, one day I would turn and seek His face through the murk and the mire, the pit of desolation I was entrenched in. In His sovereign plan for me, He knew that I would reach out to Him, open His Holy Word and read, "I waited patiently for the Lord; He turned to me and heard my cry. He lifted me out of the slimy pit, out of the mud and mire; He set my feet on a rock and gave me a firm place to stand. He put a new song in my mouth, a hymn of praise to our God. Many will see and fear (with great reverence) and will put their trust in the Lord" (Psalm 40:1–3 AMP).

What the world has to offer is a lie and eternal separation from God. It is death masked as pleasure, satisfaction, wealth, security, and even as love. Those things that are of the world are temporal with eternal consequences attached to them. Yes, we are in the world but not of the world when we have Jesus living in our hearts. The truth, the light, and life eternal with God are found only in Him. I came to know and understand that what He has to offer us is real. It's eternal, not temporal. I didn't know the difference until the day I asked Jesus to save me and abide in my heart. I had no idea that a person could have fun, enjoyment, pleasure, abundance, security, satisfaction, love, and eternal rewards with God in their life.

What I learned from Satan, the deceiver, was a lie convincing me that I could have all the pleasures of the world and that I didn't need God to attain them. I learned as well about the consequences of those worldly pleasures with the absence of God in them. God's Word tells us, "Do not love the world or anything in the world. If anyone loves the world, love for the Father is not in them. For everything in the world—the lust of the flesh, the lust of the eyes, and the pride of life—comes not from the Father but from the world" (1 John 2:15–16 AMP). Satan, the father of lies, disguises lies as truth.

The Lord tells us, "Set your minds on things above, not on earthly things" (Colossians 3:2 AMP). And while I attained all those worldly pleasures, they were never enough to fill me, to satiate me, to give me a sense of peace and fulfillment.

The scaled eyes of the blind don't know what they're missing because they can't see. Likewise, those who are blind to the ways of God can never fully see His truth. Only God can open the spiritual eyes of the blind.

Before I came to know the Lord, I didn't know that living a Christian life and enjoying myself were possible without alcohol. I didn't realize that I could wake up the morning after a party without a horrible hangover. My idea and understanding of a party then was a worldly perspective. It wasn't until my first "party" as a Christian that I learned about them being known as fellowships. A whole new world opened up to me. There weren't any regrets the next day or guilt or loathing of myself over what I had done.

But hold on, I'm getting ahead of myself. Let me take you back to where it all began.

I had suppressed uncovering and exposing the wounds and scars of my life for many years. For reasons of fear, shame, and pain, I held back finishing this book. But I'm here right now, writing again, and finally able to share how my Lord and Savior brought me to this time and place through trials and devastation. It has served to bring Him honor, praise, glory, and thanksgiving. I'm writing to encourage others and point them to Jesus, the author and perfecter of our faith. What He has done for me, He can do for you! So get in. Hang on. Strap in. We're going for a ride!

CHAPTER 3

That No Good, Cotton-Pickin' Summer

I came from a family of six. I had three other siblings and was the third of four kids in our household. Our father was a preacher's son, and our mother's parents raised her in a home with strong fundamental Christian values and beliefs. I was exposed to Christianity a few short years when I was very young. However, after events that led my parents to stray from God, I was introduced to a different world, a world without God as the center of our lives. The strength of our family unit mutated from serving God to serving self. I'll be sharing much more about the subject of self and its toxic ramifications further on.

We had a strong family work ethic, growing up in our home. Anyone who complained about working hard quickly learned it was not tolerated. During our summers, my parents took us to work in the fields, picking cotton or grapes, and to the packing sheds cutting fruit. That was how we earned money for school clothes.

We were out in the fields before sunrise and worked until sunset. When we picked cotton, I remember riding on my dad's burlap sack as I was still too young to have my own sack. Those were the summers I recall being the last "fun" cotton-picking summers in my life. All too soon, the consecutive summers enlisted me as part of the workforce wherever the work took us.

The cotton was so soft and snowy white. But its beauty had a dark side.

EVIE G.

I recall the pain of bleeding fingers and dry, cracked cuticles. Etched in my memory is the sting of scratches from the sharp razor-like tips on the rigid outer shells of the cotton balls. As carefully as I tried not to slice my skin open with each chunk of cotton I pulled, there was no escaping the inevitable. Crying or trying to throw a tantrum was counterproductive and a mute issue within my family's work ethic. I bore the fear and the pain because each cotton ball held the promise of new clothes or shoes for school. So I endured. And my father never let us forget why we needed to pick that cotton.

I was either dodging yellow jackets in the grape vineyards, cutting peaches until I couldn't open or close my aching fingers, or forcing myself to remember why I was earning money with every job we worked at. That was always on my mind.

But then came that one summer (when I was ten or eleven years old) and the raging meltdown.

It happened in the cotton field. It was the hottest, most scorching summer I had ever experienced out in the fields. The air felt so hot and thick that I couldn't catch my breath. I finally fell to my knees and began screaming wildly. My parents ran toward me, and by the time they got to me, I was sobbing so hard I couldn't speak. They tried to touch me, but I raised up and screamed at my dad. I didn't care if he hit me or anything else at that fiery, tilting moment. I yelled at him, telling him that I hated this! I told him I couldn't do this anymore, and I hated, hated, hated it!

I'll never forget that pivotal event that changed my perspective and way of thinking. Strangely enough, that was the day that I'd thank my dad about for the rest of my life. My emotional experiences with my father had vacillated between love and hate for several years. I was like a cargo train carrying baggage, waiting to derail over a cliff at any time. I'll get to the many reasons why later on.

He stood there looking down at me with what I perceived to be the slightest little grin, as though he was oddly pleased to hear what I was screaming at him. Then he said, "Good! I'm glad you don't like it! I hope you remember how much you hate it. And maybe you'll go to school and get an education so you won't have to work like this the rest of your life!"

He shocked the baggage right out of me. I stopped crying. I just sat there, slumped down with my mouth wide open as he turned his back and walked away, back to his cotton sack.

I was livid with him for that. In time, however, I would come to appreciate the wisdom of his hard and burly lesson. I remembered that day in the cotton field as I later did indeed pursue an education and became an educator in public schools.

I learned a great truth that day in the cotton field. I didn't understand then why my father made me endure such hard lessons or why he disciplined me when I tried to complain. But I would come to understand and learn how, like parents, our heavenly Father teaches us through hardships and burly lessons of life as well. He disciplines us because His wisdom and plan for us is always for our good. We find that truth in His Word: "Blessed is the one whom God corrects; so do not despise the discipline of the Almighty. For He wounds, but He also binds up; He injures, but His hands also heal" (Job 5:17–18 NIV).

I had no idea how my childhood experience in the workforce would additionally serve to teach me about being a good steward of what God gives me. Hard work reaps rewards. At times they are personal and intrinsic. Other times they are a blessing to others, and we see the fruit of our labor in God's purposes. It would also resonate with me in my walk with God when I learned to develop a heart of gratitude for my Lord and Savior in both hard times and good times.

But I'll *never* forget that cotton-pickin' summer!

Before my parents walked away from church, and as a very young child, when we weren't working or going to school, we practically lived in the church my grandfather pastored. At times it seemed as though we attended services almost every day of the week! We were a part of that congregation until a series of events happened, and we moved away to another town.

In those early years before we moved, most all of my extended family attended our church. Innocent and naive, I believed that all the adults in our family could walk on water and part the sea. I loved participating in church with them, although I would sometimes fall asleep in the pew or on the floor at my mother's feet. She always laid a coat or a blanket down for me when I could no longer keep my eyes open. Those are good memories, and I thank God for them.

However, all the illusions about some of my beloved adult family members were soon to be shattered.

One heartbreaking day, I would learn that my grandfather, our pastor, whom I idolized and loved with all my heart, was no longer living with my grandmother. Behind whispers in a conversation between my parents, I heard them say that he had left the church. I remember riding home in the back seat of our car and listening to my parents arguing. My mom was crying and talking to my dad about "that woman."

That was the beginning of my young life changing into one of growing confusion and, eventually, hate. That was the beginning of a cancerous root of bitterness growing in and polluting my heart.

When we think about what a root is, it is that part of the plant that is hidden underground, and invisible to the world. It's camouflaged. Satan can cultivate a root of bitterness in our heart where no one can see it. And if left unchecked, it pollutes our soul (mind, body, and emotions). "See to it that no one falls short of God's grace; that no root of bitterness springing up trouble you, and by it be defiled" (Hebrews 12:15 NIV).

The spiritual battle for my soul was birthing.

I couldn't wrap my head around my grandfather leaving my grandmother and the church for another woman. I didn't understand any of it. People branded him for it the rest of his life. To my joy, he stayed in our lives albeit always uncomfortable and a sorrowful situation for him and some members of my family.

The ill treatment of my grandfather went on for years, but all I ever felt for him was love and sadness. Amid all the whispers and unforgiveness toward him by most everyone, he and I maintained a loving and strong relationship with each other. He always treated me with love and never did anything to hurt me.

It was painful to see my grandfather rejected by those he loved. Much later in life, I would learn about the consequences of sin and understand its devastating cause and effect in our lives.

Eventually, my parents stopped taking us to church all together.

Charles H. Spurgeon said it well: "As the salt flavors every drop in the Atlantic, so does sin affect every atom of our nature. It is so sadly there that if you cannot detect it, you are deceived."

That's how Satan works. He is a stealth cultivator of sin.

Everything changed in our family dynamic. My father became physically and emotionally abusive to my mother. He also began leading an adulterous life. My siblings and I witnessed firsthand what our mother endured at the hands of our father. And when we would plead for him to stop abusing her, we would become targets of his abuse as well.

"Shhh, don't tell. Don't speak. You have no voice."

Sadly, in my Hispanic culture as I was growing up, children and women were to be seen and not heard. We had no voice, and we did not speak of family things in public. We were never to uncover what happened behind our "closet home."

That's what Satan does. That's how Satan works. He perverts the truth of God's Word, which tells us to love one another. "This is my commandment, that you love one another as I have loved you." (John 15:12 NIV).

What happened behind closed doors stayed there. The truth and ugliness of family secrets was like an accursed code that was "understood" and never violated by family members to the outside world. And I—I always got in trouble for acting countercultural to that norm.

That's the way Satan operates—in the dark.

Rage and disgust became my constant companions as I grew up in that environment. My childlike perspectives and all the good things I had learned in church from the adults I idolized slowly began to disintegrate. Ideal versus real became increasingly evident to me. I began to question what I had learned in church about God and His love. I began to question what I had learned about His protection.

A cancerous anger started to take hold and grow in my heart. In the midst of this turmoil and doubt about God, I then experienced a horror that no child should ever endure. My father made me a victim of his sexual abuse.

It happened when I was eight years old, and my dad called to me from his bedroom. My mom was shopping, and I was home alone with him. When she came home, in the paralysis and fear of my molestation taking place, I screamed for help and broke away from him. When I ran to her, sobbing uncontrollably and trying to tell her what my dad had been doing to me, she didn't—couldn't—believe me. But what she then said to me left me even more emotionally devastated.

She asked me what "I" had done to "make him do that," then ordered me to my room.

I remember feeling like my head was going to explode and wanting to vomit, shaking with cold growing deep in my bones.

While I was in my room terrified at what might happen next, I could hear my parents screaming and arguing behind their closed bedroom door. I was waiting for my mom to come and comfort me, talk to me, and tell me that she believed me, that it wasn't my fault, and that she was going to punish my dad for what he had done to me.

She never came.

I cried myself to sleep in a fetal position hearing her words echoing in my mind, asking me what *I* had done to make him do those things to me. It was never mentioned again. After that, I became the child who was beaten the most, and my voice became completely silenced because of the shame and guilt I was made to feel.

The whirling questions in my mind made me wonder how they could both blame me for something I might have done to "make my dad" molest me. Is that what was happening? Was it really my fault? That's how Satan, the father of lies, infiltrates and violates our hearts and minds. Doubt and confusion are two of his weapons. No one ever found out what my father had done to me. I never realized that I had been victimized. I lived believing that I was a bad girl and that all of it had somehow been my fault.

That is what Satan does. "He roams the earth like a roaring lion seeking whom he might devour" (1 Peter 5:8 NIV). He comes to destroy our lives. "The thief comes only to steal and kill and destroy; I have come that they may have life and have it to the full" (John

10:10 NIV). He especially tries to subvert God's plan for His children, wreaking havoc in their lives and doing his evil best to rob them of any security and peace. But God is always working for our good behind the scenes of our lives in the spiritual realm where the real battles are waged against us. He tells us in His Word that "no weapon that is formed against you shall prosper" (Isaiah 54:17 NASB). The battles are God's, and He will gain the victory for us. That we can count on.

When God has His hand upon our lives, anything He takes us through or allows us to experience will never be more than we can handle. He is faithful. He will always give us way of escape. He won't allow us to be tested or tempted beyond our ability to endure or resist. "No temptation has overtaken you except what is common to mankind. And God is faithful; He will not let you be tempted beyond what you can bear. But when you are tempted, He will also provide a way out so that you can endure it" (1 Corinthians 10:13 NIV).

It may not seem like He's with us during those times; it may feel like He's abandoned us and doesn't care about our pain; but in His sovereignty, He is forging us through the fire to be His vessels by design. His strength enables us to withstand and overcome the lies and deceptions of Satan for God's divine plan and purpose.

Before I asked Jesus into my heart, I didn't see or understand that. Previous to loving Him, I was too busy shaking my fist at Him and blaming Him. I once was blind to the workings of the Holy Spirit. But one day, God's love restored my sight, healed my blinded eyes, and now I see. It's clearer to me now what was meant by the saying, "If it doesn't kill you, it'll make you stronger." However, getting through the "kill you" part is never easy and doesn't make very happy campers in the process.

CHAPTER 4

The Lies of Satan Are Alive and Well

During those turbulent years of fear, hate, and confusion, life went on, and I continued to survive in our dysfunctional lifestyle of dark secrets and hidden closets. My dad continued to physically abuse us and remain unfaithful to our mother. Behind closed doors, we all walked on eggshells around him. We never knew what might trigger his anger and cause us to suffer the consequences of further beatings.

He had one affair after another. I remember overhearing my mom and aunts talking about men, and it was never anything good. Men were to be feared, and their women had to submit to them like servants. That was the twisted norm in our gene pool. If they beat their wives and were unfaithful to them, they were told by the elder women that they had to endure it. Their justification was "that's the way men are, and we have to live with it."

That has never been God's plan or design for a family unit. He tells us in His blueprint of life—His Word—the antitheses of that. "Husbands, love your wives [seek the highest good for her and surround her with a caring, unselfish love], just as Christ also loved the church and gave Himself up for her" (Ephesians 5:25 AMP). Satan's tactics, lies, and deceptions were alive and engrained in our family construct. We lived in fear.

Later in life as a Christian, I would learn something about fear. I saw an acronym about it. It said that we have two choices regarding fear:

We can:
*F*ace the
*E*nemy
*A*nd
*R*un
Or we can:
*F*ace the
*E*nemy
*A*nd
Rise!

I would learn through God's Word how to face the enemy and rise in the battles that lay ahead of me.

Women in our family were enculturated to stand by their man, even if it was on their knees in total submission to their husband's conduct and ill treatment of them. Once married always married. God's plan has always been for marriage (the way He designed it) to be for as long as they both shall live. But in a world without God's precepts at the center of marriage, we ruin what God meant to be a holy and loving union.

Abused, cheated on, silenced, and subjugated, it mattered not. We were to be at their feet and beckon call and maintain the cyclical code of silence, surrendered to lies. In the secular world, all too often, this is how life is framed when God isn't at the center of the family unit.

God never designed marriage or the lives of children to be like that. I would come to know what God's Word said about His original, loving, and honoring plan for marriage between a man and a woman. I would come to learn and love His precepts about husbands, wives, and children. But I didn't know those things at that juncture of my journey. I swore as a sadly, mixed-up teenager, however, that I would never live like that if I ever got married—famous last words.

In my culture, men were privileged. Women were martyrs and were expected to run around barefoot, pregnant, and silent. As I grew, as did my anger, hatred, and objections, I always got in trouble for rebelling against that. I paid for it every time. I never learned the easy way out by keeping my opinion and objections to myself.

It was during the beatings when I felt that the anger and resentment being lashed out on me was because of my rebellious nature toward my parents. I often heard them refer to me as the "black sheep" of the family. I didn't really know what grown-ups meant by that. But as a young child, I heard it said by people when they spoke negatively about someone. It hurt deeply. I resented them even more for ridiculing me that way.

I learned to build a hard shell around my heart to protect my sanity. God strengthened me even though I was unaware of His hand upon my life then. But nothing is hidden from the Lord. I didn't know that I was His treasured possession until one day I read, "For You formed my innermost parts; You knit me [together] in my mother's womb. I will give thanks and praise to You, for I am fearfully and wonderfully made" (Psalm 139:13–14 AMP).

CHAPTER 5

We Learned to Walk on Eggshells

My sister, who was born six years after me, was just a baby when we moved from my grandparent's acreage to another town. During those years, my dad was sometimes very kind and loving to all of us, and then something would happen to anger him, and my mom and the rest of us would pay for it. Those were ugly, painful, confusing, bitter, and tumultuous years.

To the world outside our four walls, my dad was the life of the party at family gatherings. He knew how to make everyone laugh. He would give anyone the shirt off his back. There wasn't a more generous, loving man to others than our father in everyone's eyes. People loved and even admired him.

But behind closed doors at home, it was another world—a dark world full of pornography, abuse, and hidden family secrets.

The men in our family all seemed to have a code of silence that was understood. They covered each other's back. But what they did behind veiled doors was revolting and from the pit of hell. The things that happened to me and other females in my extended family at their hands were orchestrated by men without God in their hearts.

Satan never sleeps. In time and by the power of the shed blood of Jesus, I would learn how to fight on my knees and bind the enemy! You see, the battles that are waged for our souls in the unseen realm are where we must take our stand on our knees. For the battles are spiritual. "This is not a wrestling match against a human opponent.

We are wrestling with rulers, authorities, the powers who govern this world of darkness and spiritual forces that control evil in the heavenly world" (Ephesians 6:12 GW).

One afternoon when I was a teenager and my parents were shopping in town, I was alone in our house. An uncle known for being a womanizer came to visit us. Realizing I was alone, he backed me into a corner and tried to molest me. When I fought back and told him I was going to tell my parents what he was trying to do to me, it scared him enough to beg me not to tell, and he left as fast as he could. There were no cell phones in those days, and I had to wait until my parents returned home to tell them what had happened.

They never did anything about it, and it was never mentioned again.

Evidence of the "code" was at work once again. Satan's evil scheme is to dismantle the family unit and sever the sensitivities of society. That's what he does.

CHAPTER 6

My Divine Appointment with Forgiveness

Fast forward many years, and I was attending my sister's wedding. That uncle was there. I already had two granddaughters. They were five and six years old. Keenly on guard against that uncle, I kept a close eye on him and the girls' whereabouts.

Before I knew it, across the reception hall, I could hear him calling them over to him. He was trying to entice them to come and play with the microphone he was holding as he was setting up the sound system for the wedding reception. And they, pure and innocent, totally thrilled at the prospect of singing with the microphone, went running to him.

When I saw it happening, it was like a scene in the movies where a person sees something dangerous about to happen, and suddenly they scream, legs and arms go into slow motion, and they can't move any faster because they're stuck in slo-mo. In an instant, they reached him, and I saw his hands reaching for my older granddaughter's backside. God forgive me, but if I could have electrocuted him long distance with that microphone in his hand, I would have! God was still working on some of my "rough edges."

I knew I couldn't reach them in time to stop his intended fondling, so I screamed their names across the auditorium. Everyone in the room, including my uncle, froze. I shot across the room and was at their side in a nano-second—more like a "Nana-second," truth be told. My uncle was petrified when he looked into my eyes. Quietly and gently, I told the girls to go to their mom.

When my granddaughters were out of hearing range, I turned to my petrified uncle and burned my words of warning into every fiber of his being.

I told him that I wasn't young and innocent or defenseless anymore. I threatened him, branding him with the fact of what I would do to him if he even so much as talked, let alone touched my granddaughters as long as he lived.

He mumbled something unintelligible as he tried to end the conversation. But instead, I ended it by telling him that he couldn't hurt me anymore, and I wouldn't hesitate to put him in jail if he ever went near my granddaughters again. I informed him that I would let everyone know what he had done to me, adding that I would also never forgive him for it—famous last words again.

Many years later, that uncle was in a convalescent home. God took me to a divine appointment with my uncle (as I would discover later). He had suffered a stroke, was partially paralyzed, and had multiple other health issues. I had promised my aunt, his wife, that I would go pray for him and was to meet her at the convalescent home at noon.

As I sat in the waiting area, I went back in time and recalled that dreadful day when he tried to molest me. Now here I was waiting to see him, pray for him, and slowly God revealed a horrible truth to me.

I hadn't ever forgiven him after all those years. *What now?* I thought. I dismissed it. I didn't want to think about it. It brought conviction, and I just couldn't deal with it right now, I reasoned. As I sat waiting for my aunt to arrive, I tried to distract myself by watching people entering and exiting the building. But I kept hearing that small still voice whispering to me that I hadn't forgiven him.

In one of my attempts to ignore the conviction that was beginning to overtake me, I noticed three ladies enter one of the rooms and heard them praying, then singing worship songs.

I was the worship leader at our church, and my soul was always filled with music. I was so drawn to that room by their singing. I felt the Holy Spirit nudging me to get up and go sing to the lady in that room. I hesitated. The Holy Spirit, abiding in my heart, was saying, "Go!" but the flesh was saying, "You talkin' to *me*?" This was one of those smiles and chuckle moments that God knew would come to Him in my life one day.

In my carnal mind, I reasoned it might buy me some time if I *did* go into that room. Time away from having to go into my uncle's room and deal with what every cell in my body was telling me not to deal with seemed like a good alternative at the time. Needless to say, I was (and still am) a work in progress. These things serve to remind me that God wasn't and isn't done with me yet.

What Satan means for evil, God will turn around for good. "You planned evil against me; God planned it for good to bring about the present result" (Genesis 50:20 HCSB). The Lord would reveal His orchestrated plan for me in due time.

My aunt was already thirty minutes late, and I did not want to be alone in my uncle's room with him. So with wrong motives and carnal intent for self-preservation and emotional well-being, I got up and headed to that lady's room where the singing was coming from.

What I didn't realize was that God had planned my day, my steps, and my path for another lesson in His sanctification process for me.

He was progressively transforming me with another teachable moment in humility, forgiveness, reflection, and obedience.

I stepped into that lady's room and immediately felt the presence of God's Holy Spirit. I opened my mouth and heard words coming out. I introduced myself and told them that the Holy Spirit had compelled me to their room. I heard myself sharing God's Word with them. And in obedience to the Lord, in spite of my*self*, I started worshipping God in song.

We prayed together, perfect strangers, but most assuredly, sisters in the Lord. Something wonderful happened in my soul within those moments. I entered that room one way and left it with a changed heart.

As I sat back down in the waiting area still not seeing any sign of my aunt, I went before the Lord in prayer. I acknowledged my sin of unforgiveness, repented of it, thanked God for revealing it, and asked Him to forgive me.

Praying for strength, I asked God to help me in what I needed to do. Right then and there, my aunt's absence no longer mattered. What mattered was being obedient to God and doing His will.

When I walked into my uncle's room, I looked at him with different eyes for the first time in many years. We talked. I fed him when his lunch tray arrived. And afterward, ever so gently, I asked him to forgive me for hating him all those years. And I told him that I forgave him for what he had done to me. I made peace with him even though he never responded or acknowledged his sin against me. Even so, before I left, I held his hand and prayed for him. To this day, however, I regret not having asked him if he knew Jesus as his personal Savior.

My aunt never came. When I called her later that evening, she was appalled at how she had totally forgotten that we were to have met for lunch with my uncle. But you see, that day was meant to be a divine appointment between my uncle, God, and me.

God's ways are not our ways. And His thoughts are higher than our thoughts. "For my thoughts are nothing like your thoughts," says the Lord. "And my ways are far beyond anything you could imagine" (Isaiah 55:8 NLT). The intrinsic rewards of pleasing God by our obedience far outweigh any discomfort or reluctance we may have in doing His will. When we obey the Holy Spirit, God's purposes and will are made manifest in our lives and in the lives of others. "To do what is right and just is more acceptable to the Lord than sacrifice" (Proverbs 21:3 NIV).

My uncle died shortly thereafter when a second stroke took his life. God's will for my edification was done in my heart that day in my uncle's room. I learned another lesson in the experience I had in the convalescent home. It was about obedience and forgiveness. There would be more lessons to come, and it wasn't going to be fun.

CHAPTER 7

If Not for God's Grace and a Praying Grandmother

Back in time now, I was in my senior year in high school when an incident happened that set me permanently on guard for my little sister.

One day when I was in my bedroom, I heard a commotion going on in the kitchen. My dad was livid about something regarding my sister. I heard the screaming and expletives coming from my father, and my mother was pleading for my father to stop. When I ran to see what was going on, I saw my father pick up my sister and throw her across the room.

Her back hit the wall so hard that the impact broke the wall socket. I knew then that my sister's life of abuse had begun. I ran to my sister who couldn't move, and my dad went after my mom. He had never mistreated or abused my sister like he had abused us. My dad always had a soft spot for her. I had never seen either of my parents even spank her. But something happened that day, and my dad had lost control once again.

From that day on, I did all I could to protect her. But I knew that I would be leaving her behind in our house after my graduation from high school. All I could think about was graduating and getting as far away from my dad as possible—but now this.

My emotional escape from all of these things was always in my room. There were times when I lay in bed at night, and I would remember my paternal grandmother and how she knelt down by her bed and prayed.

When I was a young child, she read her Bible to me. I would visit her, and she would always tell me stories about people in the Bible. She would sing little songs to me about Jesus, and I would sing them back to her.

She told me how to fight the devil by coming against him with the blood of Jesus. She taught me that I could rebuke the devil and bind him in the name of Jesus. She prayed for me with such tenderness. I felt so safe in my grandmother's home. I missed going to church with her and watching her lead worship. That all ended for us when we moved away.

There were times when I witnessed her crying heartfelt tears when talking to God about my grandfather who had left her. Sobbing and pleading to God, she would pray for my dad and for her other children and grandchildren as well. Never once did I tell her how my dad treated us. She adored my dad, her first born son. I knew it would break her heart to hear my words about him. When she prayed for him, I could feel her love for him as she prayed.

I saw what a relationship with God looked like when I stayed at my grandmother's home. Much later in life, I would learn the scripture about raising up a child in the ways of the Lord, and when they grow old, they will not depart from them: "Train up a child in the way he should go, and when he is old, he will not depart from it" (Proverbs 22:6 AKJV). I also learned that God is a gentleman and never forces Himself on us. He gives us free will to make choices even when they're wrong. I didn't know that God had His hand on me way back then, and that one day, I would make my own choice to follow Him.

Back home at night and in my room, I had some solace in my corner of refuge when all the fear and danger slept for a while. But hate for my father's sporadic cruelty inundated my heart.

Each day held fear about what might happen to make my dad angry and cause him to come after me or any one of us. I didn't know that fear is not of the Lord. "For God has not given us a spirit of fear but of power and of love and of a sound mind" (2 Timothy 1:7 NKJV). Fear, however, was my reality at the time. I wasn't aware that without God in our lives, we are prey to be used for Satan's diabolical plans. The power of the sword of the Spirit had not yet been revealed to me by God. That would come later in my life in God's perfect timing.

We are hopeless and helpless when we walk away from God and His abode in our heart. When we turn our back on Him, we face the evil puppet master, Satan, and he will thereafter incessantly try to gain control of our soul for eternity.

Our only hope is in Christ Jesus and Him crucified. I know that I was covered by a praying grandmother, and I know that her prayers for me reached the throne of God. But that wouldn't, as they say, "get me into heaven." Ultimately, the choice had to be my own. You see, God doesn't have any "grandchildren." We are called His children. My grandmother's salvation would not bring me into His saving grace because *she* was saved. Salvation is between me and God alone and my personal surrender to Him. Growing up, I didn't have a personal relationship with Him. I knew of Him, but I didn't know Him.

When I was with my grandmother, there was something that I felt and saw in her that made my heart soften. When I sang with her, I felt joy, and I listened with an insatiable appetite to every story or scripture she would read to me.

She also told me stories about her being part Apache and Comanche and how she had learned to speak both languages growing up in the back hills of Mexico. But Spanish was the only language I ever heard her speak.

I recall one day when we were in church, she had her hands raised in the air, praising the Lord with her eyes closed. I heard her speaking a language I had never heard before. Soon, others were speaking what sounded like the same language. All I could figure out in my young mind was that they all knew Apache and Comanche too!

EVIE G.

I wouldn't know until years later that I had heard the heavenly language being uttered and that I witnessed the manifestation of the Holy Spirit in that place with the evidence of speaking in tongues. I had no idea then how significant that moment would come to be in my future, but my heavenly Father knew.

This I did know: there was something about my grandmother that melted me like butter when I was around her. I believed and trusted in her love. I felt safe with her. There was something about her "Jesus," her *Dios*, her *Espiritu Santo* that filled her eyes with love when she spoke of them.

My grandmother's prayers for my salvation reached the throne room of God. Even though she didn't live to see it, God used her to impact my life, lead me to Jesus, and save my soul. Someday when my Lord calls me home, I'm going to thank my grandmother in person for her faithful prayers and for showing me the love of Jesus.

In my own home, God had been put on the shelf, and He was there in name only. It seemed so perfunctory when my mom would pray before we ate. We went through the motions of acknowledging God. But I didn't feel that special presence all around me like when I was at my grandmother's house, and she would pray.

Something was always missing in our ritualistic prayers at home. I would find out later, as an adult, what had been missing. My journey was still unfolding. There would be many mountains to climb and valleys to cross before I would feel that presence around me that was so real at my grandmother's.

CHAPTER 8

There's Got to Be a Better Way!

For a short time after we moved to our new home, my mom would have us read a scripture from this little card holder in the shape of a loaf of bread before every meal. Soon we stopped even that ritual at the dinner table. We knew of God. My parents could even quote scripture. But we didn't "know" God or have a personal relationship with Him. The backstory about my mother's heart for the Lord that I didn't know, however, would later be revealed as time went on.

I remember having heard stories of my mother leading worship when she was a young lady in my grandfather's church. I wondered what had happened that made her change and walk away from that. I knew that at one time in her youth, she must have developed a relationship with God because people talked about how He used her greatly in church. But I only saw glimpses of that in her, and I felt there was more inside her than she allowed us to see.

When living in our home became unbearable for me after one of the beatings I took, I did the unthinkable. I told my dad that I was going to call the police and tell them about what he had done to me. He told me to go ahead because they would agree that I deserved it. I believed him. So then I told him that I was going to run away and never come back.

My parents went to my room, came out with a suitcase packed for me and said, "Go." It shocked me. It left me speechless. My dad was the master of reverse psychology. I couldn't win. Besides, I had nowhere to go. That was the end of that.

It was pitiful.

I knew in my heart of hearts there had to be a better way, a happier way of living. I saw glimpses of it when my friend would invite me to her church in the town where we had moved to. At that church, I witnessed wives being treated with respect and a kind of tenderness. Their husbands seemed to cherish them. Their wives exuded joy when they stood next to their husbands. Those visits, infrequent as they were, left a picture imprinted in my young mind and gave me a sense of hope that there was indeed another way of living, a better, happier way to live.

It felt so good to feel that small spark of hope once in a while. Yet I couldn't help but wonder if they were like us, one face in public and another at home behind closed door. Satan, the master of deception, knows how to invade our thoughts with doubt and distrust. He is, after all, the father of lies. "When he lies, he speaks what is natural to him, for he is a liar and the father of lies and half-truths" (John 8:44 AMP).

I didn't want to give in to those thoughts. I so liked what I saw in those Christian families that I dared hope there was truly another way of living in a marriage and another way of treating children than what I had experienced in our home.

Nothing changed for the better in our household. All I longed for was the day I could leave. I didn't know then that everything Satan meant for evil and for my destruction, God was working behind the scenes to turn around for my good. No one can outdo God in His divine plan for us. "You intended to harm me, but God intended it for good to accomplish what is now being done, the saving of many lives" (Genesis 50:20 NIV). That's how God works.

God was faithfully working out His plan for my life. He promises us in His Word that He'll never give us any trial or tribulation more than we can handle, and if He does, He'll make a way of escape. "Every test that you have experienced is the kind that normally comes to people. But God keeps His promise, and He will not allow you to be tested beyond your power to remain firm; at the time you are put to the test, He will give you the strength to endure it and so provide you with a way out" (1 Corinthians 10:13 GNT).

My high school years were a whirlwind of emotions. In my senior year, I couldn't wait to escape the house and leave my life of abuse behind. Fear gripped my every thought at what my mom and sister might continue to go through after I left.

My whole life up to that point had been one of fighting to survive my circumstances. I hadn't yet learned how to fight on my knees and seek God to help me through my fears—not then, not yet.

My oldest brother was off to college and living away from home. My other brother and I were in our last year of high school. He would leave for Vietnam shortly after graduation. And I—I was a teenager who was an angry, resentful, emotional, oncoming train wreck!

I didn't want my younger sister to suffer what I had, and I racked my brain trying to figure out how to protect her from our dad. I lived for the day I could get away, find someone who would love me, not abuse me, someone that I could marry someday, hoping that I would have the kind of marriage that I saw in those Christian families from my childhood.

CHAPTER 9

The Day of Imploding Reckoning

That day came. I was going to break free at last. Straight out of high school and in my first year of junior college, I met and fell head over heels in love with an airman stationed at a nearby air force base. After only four months of dating, we set the date and planned our wedding. I swore to myself that my life and the lives of our future children would be different—better, safer, happy.

On my wedding day, before I left my house and with every ounce of courage I could muster, I confronted my father.

All the seething anger, all the horrid memories of abuse, all the rage and hate, all the years of having the hope beaten out of me, came to a head. I took my dad aside, and my emotional volcano erupted! I warned him in no uncertain terms that if he ever tried to sexually abuse my little sister like he had abused me, I wouldn't keep quiet, and I would make sure he went to jail.

He raised his hand to strike me, and I told him that I wouldn't be silent. I would tell everyone about him. He never said a word to me after that. He lowered his hand to his side. He must have seen something in my eyes that convinced him that I meant every word. He never touched my little sister in any way after that. She graduated high school and left home unscathed by my father.

After my sister graduated high school—an empty nest in my parent's lives—my father went from bad to worse. "For from within, out of the heart of man, come evil thoughts, sexual immorality, adultery, wickedness, sensuality. All these evil things come from within, and they defile a person" (Mark 7:21–23 ESV).

My mom called me one day and told me that dad was being accused of molesting a little girl from a family we knew. He did so on the same bed he had molested me. Charges were brought against him, but he was never convicted. I remembered the "code" and wondered if there was a similar code for all men back then. Satan is a master at building strongholds in the heart of man. How my dad wasn't convicted, I'll never know. My mom was silent after that.

When our lives are gripped by strongholds, they can take over our hearts. It's only when we surrender our lives to Jesus that we can have victory over our strongholds. But I was to learn in God's Word that there is a Chain Breaker, a Way Maker, and a Stronghold Busting Savior. And His name is *Jesus*!

How evident would that truth come to be for me in the trials and temptations to come.

My husband and I had made a life for ourselves, and we had two precious children. Our lives were all that I'd ever hoped for in the first few years of our marriage. But I came to a place in time where I had to make a decision for myself.

My well-being and state of mind were still full of unrest regarding my dad and our relationship. I couldn't shake the whirling emotions spinning in my mind about him. I decided to go see him. I had purposed in my heart that I needed to break free from the past and release it somehow. Through tears and at times not being able to breathe from the emotion pouring out of me, he agreed to meet with me. I shared my heart with him. I told him how he had devastated my life when I was growing up in our home. I confessed that I hated him for years because of what he had done to me and our family. But this time, instead of threatening him, I told him that I had come to release the past, that hatred, and forgive him.

I explained how the rage, hate, and pain of it still plagued me and was destroying my emotional health.

Even though I was not a Christian at the time, I remembered seeing love and forgiveness in my grandmother's ways. I wanted that kind of peace, that kind of heart. I told him that I couldn't live with that hatred anymore. It was affecting my daily life, and I needed to move forward and free myself from its grip.

As I poured out my heart out to him, I didn't know that the Master Weaver was at work in my soul, weaving His tapestry of design for my life.

Anger and hate are twin sins that can consume us when we are bound by them. They are strategic weapons of the enemy of our soul. They are poison. They are toxic waste that he uses to pollute our lives with the sole intention of destroying our peace. They were consuming me like a cancer growing as wildfire within me. When it came to my dad, the pain and bitterness far outweighed those few sporadic years of "good" memories. I couldn't get past that.

I was to learn about those sister sins from God's Word. "If you forgive others the wrongs they have done to you, your Father in heaven will also forgive you. But if you do not forgive others, then your Father will not forgive the wrongs you have done" (Matthew 6:14–15 GNT).

The emotional challenge that lay before me in the presence of my dad was overwhelming. But I knew that I had to face my demons and be set free. My being there with him was so surreal—just me and him, no one around, adult to adult. But I was shaking inside, afraid I wouldn't be able to get through it all. And yet it was as though I was hovering in a bubble of protection before him, and I knew that nothing he could say or do to me could touch me. The time had come.

I told him about the battle raging within me, and he listened, really listened. I felt I was alone, on my own, with no one to defend me but myself. As I heard my words spilling out, I didn't realize that God was right there with me. I didn't think about those Sunday school classes way back then when I heard about bitterness and forgiveness. I didn't think about the lessons I had learned about God's Word never coming back void. His mercies and grace never entered my mind as I sat there with my heart raw and exposed with grief.

But He was there. Jesus was my advocate, right by my side, even though I wasn't aware of it.

He promises to never leave us or forsake us in time of need and through every ordained step of the way. We find His promise in His

Word. "Be strong and courageous, do not be afraid or tremble in dread before them, for it is the Lord your God who goes with you. He will not fail you or abandon you" (Deuteronomy 31:6 AMP).

Well I got through it. My father didn't say much when I unloaded all my grief on him. He couldn't speak when I asked him to forgive me for hating him. He just hung his head and gestured his acceptance.

He died four years later of a massive coronary.

I'm thankful that my husband, children, and I had some quality years with him before he died. Something deep within him had started to change over time, and I began to view him in a different light. He treated my mom differently, with tenderness and love. Sadly, however, I never quite felt unguarded when he was around my children. When we were all together with him, I never took my eyes off of him, and he knew it. Dad and I had a very clear and unmistakable understanding about his relationship with my children. In time, I saw that he dearly loved them, and they came to love him with all their hearts as well. I'll be forever thankful to him for that. And I thank God that mom and dad had a more loving relationship and seemed to be happy together the last few years of his life.

CHAPTER 10

The Beauty of Forgiveness

A month after my dad died, the man I idolized, cherished, and loved with all my heart died as well. My precious, beloved grandfather, my dad's father, passed away from a massive heart attack. My heart was shattered.

Before he died, God, in His mercy and grace, orchestrated a wonderful healing between my grandmother and grandfather.

Nearly a month after my dad's passing, some of us gathered at the home of my dad's sister. My grandmother was now living with her and under my aunt's care. There was a knock at the door. When I opened it, my grandfather was standing there in the doorway. He looked broken and devastated, deep in mourning at the loss of my dad, his son. But there was something more in his eyes, something else about the look on his face.

He came inside, sat down across from my grandmother as we were all sitting around the kitchen table. Tears welled up in his eyes as he reached for my grandmother's hands.

There, in front of us all, he asked her for forgiveness. He told her that he had left the other woman and had repented of his sins. We were all in tears as we witnessed the healing taking place between them. As my grandfather waited for a reply, my loving grandmother told him that she forgave him. He kissed her hand, stood up, kissed her cheek, and they embraced.

We flooded that kitchen with tears of joy in that unspeakably treasured moment. The visit lasted for a long while, and it was good. We hadn't seen my grandparents so happy together in years. God's merciful plan for them and the repentance and forgiveness in their hearts made that healing possible.

My grandfather died of a massive coronary three day later.

We had buried my dad only one month earlier. They died a month apart, and we were crushed.

God was merciful to me. He had a plan for me, and He even provided the seat belt for that even bumpier ride that was to come into my life. Unknown to me, that very act of forgiveness for others and for myself would be one of many that He had planned for me as He continued to mold me and make me into a yielded vessel for His purposes.

My cherished, loving grandmother, the one who prayed for me, who taught me the ways of the Lord, who showed me what real Christian love was, died three years after my dad and grandfather.

CHAPTER 11

The Journey Navigated by the Master's Hand

After the loss of our loved ones happening one after the other, I thought it might do my mom and I some good to get away for a while and take a long trip together. We decided to go to Washington to visit relatives there. I drove back to my hometown, got mom, and we headed out. Neither one of us being great at reading maps, we got lost a couple of times. But that was half the fun in our misguided minds. The Lord helped us find our way in more ways than one on that fateful trip. It was a very long drive, so we had a lot of time to talk on and off the road.

It was during that trip that another wonderful healing would take place.

We were driving along, talking and enjoying the sights. The kids were fast asleep in the back seat of the car. Mom suddenly became very quiet. I looked over at her in the passenger seat next to me and noticed her head hung down as she burst into tears. My immediate thought was that she was thinking about my dad and our loss of loved ones.

She was sobbing so uncontrollably that I pulled over to the side of the road. She couldn't speak and was having trouble catching her breath. I calmed her down and wrapped my arms around her, reassuring her and telling her to let it out and cry. I told her that it was going to be all right.

After she calmed down, I asked her what it was that was happening to her. What she said to me was nothing I could have ever imagined she had been thinking.

When she was able to speak, she reached for my hand, looked into my eyes, and through a flood of tears, asked me to forgive her.

I was perplexed, confused, and asked her what she was talking about. She asked me to forgive her for not defending me when my dad molested me.

She told me that she had been a coward. I couldn't bear to hear her refer to herself like that. I tried to stop her from saying more, but she made me listen to her.

Trembling and inconsolable, she told me that she hadn't been able to forgive herself all those years for not having done something about it. She shared how she couldn't take the guilt and shame any longer for not speaking up in my defense.

Looking deep into my tear-filled eyes, she told me that she had been afraid to be on her own with all of us kids and not be able to survive without my dad's support. She knew that it might happen if she spoke up against him.

Through my precious mother's tears, she shared that for years, she had wanted to ask me to forgive her, but she was ashamed and afraid to ask me.

The strangest thing happened in that moment. As I gazed into her eyes, I saw my grandmother's tender and loving eyes of forgiveness looking back at me.

We both broke down through tears of release. I told my mom that I loved her and that I had forgiven her long ago. We held each other for a long, long time. There was a sweet presence that flooded our souls, and she knew that all was well between us. It was God working in the unseen realm, bringing healing once again. And I still didn't recognize His hand at work in me—not yet.

I'm tellin' ya, the Potter had His work cut out for Him when He took this clay of His named Evie, and started workin' me into His design. He took me, just a lump of clay in His hands. He was molding me, forming me on His Potter's wheel of life. He pulled me here and pulled me there. Sometimes He had to pull off the lumps and bumps that interfered with His design for me. So many times, He had to smooth out the imperfections in this vessel as He fashioned me into His image and design.

At times it hurt deeply when He added or subtracted from His creation in progress. But slowly, yieldingly, this clay began to respond to the Potter's hands. A vessel unworthy, so full of sin. But He did not throw this clay away when this vessel broke.

He just picked up the pieces and started over again. Like that old song says, "You see the Potter, He knows the clay and how much pressure it can take." The Potter is patient and knows what it will take to fashion a vessel that He can use. I was and am a work in progress, no doubt about it.

Over the years, after I was serving the Lord, the relationship with my mom developed into an even deeper and more cherished one. God continued to bless our times together. We both loved the Lord with all our heart. We took many trips, including a cruise to Alaska, together. No matter where we traveled, singing praises to our Lord was always a part of our journeys together. I came to know that part of her that she kept suppressed all those years married to my dad. I saw that worship leader in her bloom once again and the joy all over her face when we would sing the songs we used to sing in my grandfather's church. I finally saw my mom happy.

CHAPTER 12

The Devil Dancing on My Grave

God's plans for us are always good. Just as God used Joseph's brothers and King Saul to carry out His plans through adversity, He would use my adversities to unfold His good and perfect will for my life as well.

Before I became a Christian, the Lord wanted me to see the spectrum of the world's view regarding Him and compare it to what I saw in my own family. I saw parallel similarities. By comparison, we can think of the human race as a sort of family. There are multitudes of values, religions, and beliefs in our world just as there are within families.

God showed me that within my own family, there were those who demonstrated a true and abiding relationship with God. I could tell because they were "different." I saw it in what they said or didn't say, what they did or didn't do, in public and in private. They were in the world, but not of it.

There were also those who were religious. But they did not walk with God and lacked a personal relationship with Him. They attended church religiously.

Then there were others in our family who partied, drank, did drugs, cheated on their spouses, and were in the world and of it as well.

I lived in and around all of those environments.

I would learn through it all how God can turn what seems like random chaos into strategic, targeted norm for His divine purposes in our lives. Nothing that He allows us to experience is without His divine purpose in mind. My experiences in my immediate family were like being in a world within a world. God helped me to see that life within or outside our family, without Him in it, will have chaos as its epicenter.

Home life had always colored my world with darkness and despair for many years growing up. I suppressed the teachings of my grandmother because hope wasn't alive and well in my heart.

My life was on a road named Disaster, and the ride I was on promised to have many more twists and turns that I never could have imagined. These were the years that I know made God shed those tears for me and when I broke His heart.

He knew as well how these painful but necessary adversities must be a part of my journey in His plan of salvation for me.

God, whose plans and mind we can never fully comprehend, is always working behind the scenes of our lives. He fashions the lives of those He loves for His divine purposes. It's a profound mystery that will someday be revealed to us according to His Word.

Much later, as a believer, I came to understand what Holocaust survivor, Corrie Ten Boom, said: "Don't ever be afraid to trust an unknown future to a known God."

I didn't know it then, but Matthew 7:13–14 (NIV) was going to jump right out of the Bible at me and be a floodlight to me in my darkest hours. "Enter through the narrow gate. For the gate is wide, and the road is broad that leads to destruction, and there are many who go through it. How narrow is the gate and difficult the road that leads to life, and few find it." God was leading me toward the narrow gate…

Back in Time—Backstory: the Beginning of the End

My husband, the one who I thought was going to be the answer to all my hopes and dreams, was used by the enemy of our souls, on the continuing roller coaster ride of my life. We had some very happy years together with our two children, but as the years progressed, our marriage began to disintegrate. God was not a part of our lives because neither one of us had a personal relationship with Him.

After our children were both enrolled in school, I went back to college and eventually graduated with my teaching degree. During those years of attending the university, raising our children, and before I began teaching, my husband and I led a life full of parties and alcohol.

When people are empty inside without God abiding in their hearts, they try to satisfy their carnal nature with worldly distractions. It's so very easy to get caught up in the world with all of its enticements. Distractions from God come in many forms. Sometimes it's hobbies, relationships, or money. It's even things such as cell phones, TV, and so much more. But when we fix our eyes on Jesus, our mind and priorities shift to what is eternally important:

> Set your minds on things that are above, not on things that are on earth. (Colossians 3:2 ESV)

> As we look not to the things that are seen but to the things that are unseen. For the things that are seen are transient, but the things that are unseen are eternal. (2 Corinthians 4:18 ESV)

> You keep him in perfect peace whose mind is stayed on you, because he trusts in you. (Isaiah 26:3 ESV)

Unfortunately, while temporary pleasures of the world permeate our existence, they are never quite enough to fill the void that only Christ can fill with His love. And the eternal consequences of living in the world and being of the world carries the ultimate consequence—separation from God for eternity.

My husband and I fought constantly. He smoked pot with his friends and some of my family members as well. It was always a contention between us because I was vehemently against drugs of any kind. It's funny how quickly we judge others for sinning and doing something we think is more sinful than our own sins. Sadly, it is always the perspective of the unredeemed, even of some redeemed.

To our impending destruction, my husband started having affairs with other women, but I never knew about them. Everyone else did as I would discover much later. I was the last one to know. But at one point, I suspected he was having an affair with one of our mutual female friends. I was too afraid to do or say anything about it. The thought that my husband could start being like my dad had been with my mom terrified me. I couldn't—I didn't want to believe it or accept it might be true. But that changed.

He had become increasingly distant with me, and I knew we were headed to a big conflict down the road. One of the nights, when he didn't come home after work, and it was 2:00 a.m., I did the unthinkable.

I left my sleeping children alone upstairs at home in search of my husband.

I was driving and crying so hard that I couldn't see straight. My heart was breaking like shattered glass. But I decided to face my worst fears and drove to the house of the woman I suspected he was with.

When I drove into the court where she lived, I saw his van in her driveway. At that moment, the enemy had such a hold on me, and I was so enraged with hate and pain that I could have killed them both right then and there. The things that raced through my mind were horrific.

I saw myself crashing my car into her house. I imagined plowing my car into my husband's van. I pictured myself ringing the doorbell then bursting into her home and choking her to death. I set her car and his on fire in my tortured mind's eye. I even contemplated turning my car around and racing to the freeway to end my life in a car crash.

All of these evil thoughts came flooding into my soul, and I couldn't control them.

Paralyzed with grief and fear at the thought of my children at home asleep stopped me cold. In a moment of saving clarity concerning my children, I found myself, instead, parked next to my husband's van in her driveway, sitting in my car and numb from head to toe. I would think about my children later, I reasoned. That's what Satan does.

When he has you where he wants you, what makes sense to the irrational mind seems rational to the deceived mind. That's why Satan, the enemy of our soul, is called the author of confusion. He seeks to cause chaos, disorder, pain, death, and destruction. But God gives us hope and encouragement in the midst of our trials. "For God is not the author of confusion but of peace" (1 Corinthians 14:33 NKJV).

I decided I would wait in my car until my husband came out of her house and then confront him. It felt like an eternity as I waited, sobbed, sat there, shaking from the cold and sick to my stomach with emotions.

At one point, I left my car and decided to wait for him in his van. Eventually, her front door opened, and I saw them embrace and kiss each other at her door. When he turned to leave her, he saw my car in front of her house. He turned to say something to her, then headed for my car. When he didn't see me in it, he walked over to his van door and saw me sitting in the back seat.

It was the most dreadful, painful ordeal that I had ever experienced with him. We sat in the van and talked. He told me that he loved her and wanted a divorce. I lost all senses and ran to my car. I had thoughts of suicide. I had thoughts of finding a gun and coming after both of them to kill them.

The devil was tormenting my soul and celebrating his victories over me. *He was dancing on my grave.*

But then… God!

You see when God has His hand upon your life, no one, no tragedy, no obstacle, no circumstance or situation can interfere with His ordained plan for you. He saves us from ourselves, and we don't even realize it. But He knows what His plans are for us, and they are for good in His grand scheme for our lives. He tells us in His Word, "'I know the plans I have in mind for you,' declares the Lord. 'They are plans for peace, not disaster, to give you a future filled with hope'" (Jeremiah 29:11 CEB).

It was after I bolted out of his van, got into my car, and screeched out of that court that I somehow made it home in one piece. I snapped. I fell apart. I broke into a million pieces.

After eighteen years of marriage, he told me he no longer loved me and wanted out of our marriage.

That very moment was the unravelling of all that God meant to be sacred in his original intent for our marriage. The tapestry we had woven into our lives lacked the design God had intended and created for a marriage between a man and a woman. "Marriage is to be honored by all, and husbands and wives must be faithful to each other. God will judge those who are immoral and those who commit adultery" (Hebrews 13:4 GNT).

CHAPTER 13

God, if You Exist, Where Are You?

I can't remember how I made it back home, but I found myself lying prostrate on the couch. I don't know how long I had been screaming into my tear-drenched pillow, but when it became hard to breathe, I slumped back, and my heart was aching so much that I felt like it would burst.

I heard a voice whisper in my head, "Kill yourself. End your pain. You won't hurt anymore. You'll make them pay for what they've done to you. Your kids will be okay. Don't worry about them. They'll survive and recover. Kill yourself."

The accuser, the enemy of my soul was planting the seeds of selfishness and destruction, trying to fill me with pity for myself. He didn't want me to think of my precious children and what my death would truly cause them.

Satan is indeed the master of deception and the father of lies. He had me where he wanted me, and he was wickedly dancing on my grave. He moves in when we're vulnerable, when he knows he's able to convince us of his lies. And his goal is to kill, steal, and destroy our souls.

I was spent and at the end of my rope. The pain and deception of my husband hurt too much. I couldn't take it anymore.

The man I loved, the father of my children, the one who I thought I would spend the rest of my life with, was throwing me away—us away—for another woman. I suddenly remembered my mother, how she must have felt when this happened to her, and it horrified me. It was my father all over again! What would I tell our children? How could this be happening?

Slowly, I began to feel a rage welling up inside me, a force so strong that it felt like there was an evil presence growing inside my body. I stood up, raised my clenched fist in the air, looked up, and with hate deep within my heart, I heard myself say, "There is no God! If you exist, where are you? It's a lie! Everything they said about you is a lie! I don't want to live in this world anymore! It hurts too much! Living is too much pain. Please, I just want the pain to stop."

Isn't it ironic how the unbeliever, the unredeemed, deny the existence of the very God they're yelling at and acknowledging must be listening to them? That's what deception is. That's what the accuser of the brethren does. He perverts the truth of God's Word for his diabolical, destructive purposes.

I dropped to the couch, sobbing uncontrollably. I thought about how to end my life quickly and how all the pain would stop. I wanted that. I wanted all of it to end, to be over and done with.

I pictured my husband and his affair filled with guilt in each other's arms. I saw the look of disdain on the faces of my loved ones blaming them for my suicide. It felt good, this vengeance I was feeling in the images of what it would be like for them after I was dead. It felt satisfying seeing them feeling responsible for my death.

Evil, evil most vile were the thoughts that spun in my mind as the enemy was winning his battle for my soul. That's how Satan works. He infiltrates the mind and heart of the hurting as he plots the destruction of the vulnerable.

I began to think of my children. I saw them grieving at my casket. I saw them alone, truly alone, not able to accept what I had done. The thought that they would be all right eventually without me slithered into my mind. I thought about my daughter's wedding and how I wouldn't be there for her. I thought about my son in high school and all the things I would not be there to support him in. And then other thoughts began creeping into my mind.

In the spiritual realm, the battle was raging for my soul.

Those other thoughts started to slip in between my swirling confusion. I heard the word *selfish*. I couldn't understand. I heard it again—selfish. And then I heard more words: *It's not about you. It's about others. It's about your children. It's about putting them first, not yourself. How selfish of you to think about doing that to your children.* Then came the question: What about the pain you'll give *them* if you kill yourself?

God works behind the scenes of our lives in mysterious ways so that His will might be manifested in our lives for His purposes. I know Satan and his minions must have been screaming in horror at this intervention of God's mighty hand into the battle for my soul. I was slowly, but surely, beginning to slip away from Satan's stronghold over my mind and heart.

You see, God was my deliverer, my shield, and my strength. I was covered by the anointed prayers of my grandmother and by the blood of Jesus that she prayed over me. Lucifer, who disguises himself as an angel of light, dripped his toxic drops of poison into my mind and heart. He tried to convince me that his way was the better way, the easiest way out of my pain.

But God's Word says, "But the Lord is faithful, and He will strengthen you and protect you from the evil one" (2 Thessalonians 3:3 GNT).

More evidence of God's protection and plan for my salvation was about to birth in my life in the following hours of this battle.

CHAPTER 14

Meeting the Savior of My Soul

My mind was mush. I knew I must be delirious and hallucinating because I heard that voice in my head say, "Turn on the TV." I heard it once more. The voice was so compelling and undeniable that I reached for the remote. Then another voice invaded my thoughts. "That's stupid! There's nothing on TV right now. Kill yourself and end your pain!"

Crazy, unbelievably crazy, right?

Those who are unaware of the reality of the spiritual realm are hard-pressed to believe in assertions that attest to the existence of good and evil battling for the souls of man in the unseen dimension.

Many only believe in what they see. It's what we don't see that can only be believed by *faith* and the *truth* of God's Word. My mom's father once told me, "When you hear a little voice in your head telling you what's right or wrong, listen and do what's right."

Well I found myself holding that remote in my hand, and I clicked it. Nothing about what was happening to me made sense. I just found myself "going through the motions" in a daze. I went through five channels, and there was nothing but snow and static. Undone, and as I was about to put down the remote, I clicked it one last time. Up on the screen, an image came into view. It was a man. The camera closed in on his face, and he pointed at the camera and said, "You, you haven't tuned in by accident. This message is for you. Don't touch that dial. God wants to tell you something."

Crazier still, right?

Sometimes God uses the unbelievable to confound the wise. Sometimes it takes the unbelievable to get our attention. And sometimes that's what it takes to believe in the miraculous hand of God at work before our doubting eyes.

He went on. "You've tried everything. But you haven't tried Jesus. He's the answer you're looking for. He wants to save you, free you from your sins, give you hope and life! He loves you. He wants to come into your heart and wash you white as snow, cleanse you of hate and bitterness and hopelessness. He's the answer, my friend. All you have to do is ask Him into your heart, ask Him to forgive you of your sins, and mean it with all your heart. Believe in Him. He's the Way, the truth and the Life. And He's waiting for you right now. He's waiting to change your life and give you peace—His peace—and eternal life. If that's you, don't turn off the TV. Don't change that dial. Say this prayer with me and let Jesus save you and give you a new life, my friend."

That morning, all by myself, just me, God, and that preacher, had a divine appointment. I fell to my knees, knowing it was God speaking to me, answering me through this man. Through tears of sorrow and gratitude, I repeated the prayer of salvation, asking Jesus into my heart.

All I can tell you is what happened next was indescribable. But those words that morning, that encounter with the hand of God upon my heart, will forever be etched in my soul.

I indeed died that day.

I died to the old self and was born into new life by the saving grace of God. That preacher led me in the prayer of salvation, and I gave my heart to Jesus. "I will sprinkle clean water on you and make you clean from all your idols and everything else that has defiled you. I will give you a new heart and a new mind. I will take away your stubborn heart of stone and give you an obedient heart" (Ezekiel 36:25–26 (GNT).

I would learn what God's Word says about His salvation: "Therefore, if anyone is in Christ, he is a new creation. The old has passed away; behold, the new has come" (2 Corinthians 5:17 ESV).

Overwhelmed with a torrent of tears, this time—tears of joy, hands raised, thanking God, praising His name—something else happened to me. I felt a deep and abiding peace, a peace in my heart that I had never experienced before.

And I just knew that everything was going to be all right. How? I didn't know. But this I did know: Something wonderful, inexplicable happened inside of me, and it was *real!*

As I was praising the Lord, thanking Him, and crying tears of joy, I suddenly began to feel this hot, hot sensation in my feet. I didn't understand what was happening, but I wasn't afraid. The heat traveled up my legs, to my stomach, chest, throat, raised arms, then it shot out of my hands and head, taking my breath away. When it left me, I felt like the weight of the whole world had been lifted from me.

The next thing I knew, I was jumping up and down, arms waving in the air, and these words were flowing out of my mouth. I saw a vision of my grandmother in church, waving her arms and speaking in a language I didn't recognize. I knew Spanish and English, but it was neither of them.

I heard myself speaking like my grandmother had at church in that language of Apache or Comanche! I didn't understand that the Holy Spirit had filled me with His indwelling and had given me my heavenly language as well.

But I knew that I knew that I knew, God was real, and I would never be the same. In God's Holy Word, He tells us of John the Baptist when he said, "I baptize with water those of you who have changed your hearts and lives. The One who is coming after me will baptize you with the Holy Spirit and fire" (Matthew 3:11 CEB).

I don't know how long I was lost in unspeakable joy, speaking in tongues, crying, and praising the Lord. But when God's Holy Spirit completed His work in me, the feeling of unbridled love and a heart of forgiveness flooded my soul.

CHAPTER 15

God—the Way Maker, the Healer, and Chain Breaker!

I found myself wanting to shout it to the world! I wanted to tell everyone what had happened to me! I called and woke up my husband's sister and my brother-in-law who had witnessed to me about the Lord in the past.

They were the ones who I confided in when there was trouble between my husband and me. They were the ones who pointed me to the Lord and always reminded me that He had all the answers. And they were the ones who reminded me that I had tried everything the world had to offer but had not tried Jesus.

When they understood what I was ranting and raving about and calmed me down, we celebrated and rejoiced together over the phone like firecrackers on the Fourth of July!

It was an ecstatic celebration. After things settled down somewhat, I shared the story about my husband and what I had discovered. They prayed for me and prepared me for the spiritual battle to come. And come it did.

Eventually, my husband came home that morning. I was waiting for him, and I shared what had happened to me. I told him that I forgave them both. I was as yet unaware that later in my Christian walk, I would find that *really* forgiving them both would be another mountain to climb in the battle ahead.

We talked until it was time for both of us to go to work. I asked him if he'd be willing to work on our marriage with me, and he said he would. He also told me he would stop seeing her.

We both went to work after getting our kids off to school. Neither one of us had slept. When I was at the chalkboard in my classroom about to write something, I collapsed. After a long talk with my principal in her office, she consoled me and sent me home for the day.

The ensuing year was a rough one in our marriage. My sister-in-law and her husband helped me find a Christ-centered church in town, and I began attending faithfully, but it was without my husband by my side. I listened to my pastor's counsel and kept praying for my husband's salvation. I asked my husband to participate in marriage counseling at my church. He went twice then stopped. God's truth and His plan for marriage was too much for him to accept about himself.

We stayed together for a year. It was just before Christmas when I found out that my husband had never stopped having the affair.

I confronted him about it, and he didn't deny it. He was totally unrepentant about what he had continued doing in secret behind closed doors. I wasn't crushed this time. I clung to the Lord and waited for Him to show me the way. But I was in a sort of daze each day thereafter.

We all walked on eggshells around him when he did come home. He started being abusive in his treatment and behavior both to me and our children.

It was becoming more and more fearful being around him. My mind spun like a whirlwind to the past when I was living at home, growing up. I was there again. It began to feel like the nightmare of abuse starting all over again.

I had to get us away from him and seek help. I left with my children to stay with my husband's sister and her family for support. After three days of respite, prayer, and advice from them, I headed back home with my children.

When we arrived that evening, we saw a light upstairs, so we knew he was home. We couldn't get in. Through the window, we saw he had propped a chair up against the doorknob. So my son hopped on the fence's side gate to climb over it and open it for us. But he saw boards with nails sticking up from them propped up against the gate. He found a way to get around them then let us in.

After we snuck upstairs quietly, trying to reach our bedrooms, I saw my husband sitting in that room with a shotgun in his hands. I told my children to run to their rooms and lock the doors. I was going to do the same and call the police. I truly, truly wasn't thinking straight and was in panicked, survival mode. After we were all locked in our rooms, I picked up the phone to call the police, but it wouldn't dial. He was on the other phone listening. All I could do was pray God's protection through the night. He didn't bother us that night. He left for work before the children got up.

After I woke the kids, I kept them home from school and got a substitute for my classroom. It was a Friday, and we were going to need a place to stay. We packed some clothes and whatever we could into the car.

Nowhere in God's Word does He tell us to endure abuse—spousal or otherwise—that I knew. My worst fears about abuse had eventually manifested themselves in my husband and in our home. I fled with my kids with little more than a toothbrush, some clothes, and shoes. I took us to a safe place at the home of some dear friends of ours.

My children had so many questions about our situation. As God gave me strength and as best I could, I tried to be strong for them that night. We cried in each other's arms. They finally fell asleep, and I went to the kitchen to talk to our friends, explaining in detail what had happened. They told me we could stay as long as we needed.

The will of God will never take us where the grace of God cannot keep us (author unknown). God made a way of escape for us, and I was so very thankful for that. That night as I lay next to my children, I thanked God for the shelter He had provided, and I laid my petitions at the feet of Jesus.

The next morning, I knew I would somehow need to find an apartment for us. It was all I could do to put one foot in front of the other and walk into an unknown future. Clinging to the hem of Jesus's garment, I left my children with our friends and went in search of a place for us to stay. It was Saturday, and I just know in retrospect that God led me to the place and a man from my past.

The Lord goes before us in the battles we face, preparing a path and the hearts of those He uses to make a way where there seems to be no way.

God brought to mind this realtor who had sold us our home, and I felt the leading of the Holy Spirit directing me to his office. I hadn't seen him in many years, but he was still in business, and I found his office. I know I must have looked like death warmed over when I walked into the office. My eyes were swollen, and my head was swirling from lack of sleep from the night before. My stomach was tied up in knots from having to face the same man who had sold us our home and tell him what had happened. When I walked in, his secretary took one look at me and told me I needed an appointment.

That's all it took.

Tears came pouring down my face, and I slumped down onto the chair next to me. Through gasps of trying to catch my breath, I asked her to please tell him my name and that he was our realtor who sold us our house several years ago.

She consoled me then went into his office. Within seconds, they came out, he took one look at me, put his arms around me, and took me into his office. I was embarrassed, ashamed, humiliated, and undone. Having to tell him what had happened stripped me of all pride. I didn't want my marriage and our private lives in the community to be exposed as a lie for all to see. But the Lord gave me the courage to fight for myself and for my children to give us a better life than the one we had been living.

As we talked in his office, he asked me what he could do to help us. I told him I needed to find an apartment as soon as possible. He reluctantly informed me that he had nothing available at that moment. He told me to wait just a minute, then he left his office to speak to his secretary. I wanted to run away. I wanted to scream. I wanted to disappear. I wanted to wake up and find that this was all just a horrible nightmare.

Millions of thoughts coursed through my mind. I started asking God, "Where are You, Lord? I thought You brought me here. Please, Father, help me trust You right now. Please, give me Your peace."

He came back into his office, sat down, and told me the situation. He did have one apartment, but it wasn't ready to rent yet. This was the month of December and very cold. He told me the heater didn't work, but he could have it fixed the following Monday. He said it was only a one-bedroom apartment, but if I wanted it, we could move in tomorrow. I broke down, feeling as though I would pass out, then he came over to me. He told me not to worry about first and last month's rent or deposit costs. We could discuss and take care of that later.

Who does that?—only God, only God, only *God!* When God opens a door, no man can close it. He makes a way where there seems to be no way. That's why He's called the Way Maker, the Healer, and the Chain Breaker. He softens the hearts of others to do His will for those He loves and are His treasured possessions.

Faith and trust—another one of God's lessons for me, another "valley" He would take me through. His plan continued to unfold in my life with new mercies every morning. He takes the pain out of our adversities and replaces them with joy, regardless of the circumstances that seem without resolve. He teaches us to be thankful even in heart-wrenching hardships.

With newfound hope, I thanked him and thanked God for hiding us in the shelter of His arms.

The things of this world seem so deceivingly important to us. We had a two-story house, swimming pool, and spa, a four-bedroom home, and lived in a wonderful neighborhood. We had the cars, the bank accounts, and all the things of the "good life" we could possibly want. But we didn't have Jesus. Satan, the enemy of our souls, destroyed our false sense of security and our family. But you see, we let him.

He blinds us to the truths of God and perverts our priorities into believing his lies. The things of this world are temporal and deceiving. If we let him, without even knowing it more often than not, Satan gets a foothold, then soon that becomes a stronghold, and we become blind to the eternal importance of our lives. With God's mercy and provision, my children and I moved into our apartment the next day.

That night, I used the oven in the kitchen to warm us through the night. The following day, when my husband was at work, we went home, got blankets, pillows, and clothes. I remember crying in the kitchen of our home while the kids were upstairs, getting their things together. I couldn't believe it had come to this.

I took three spoons, three forks, three knives, three plates, and just enough of what we needed to get us through. As I counted each of those things in groups of three, it hit me so very hard. We were now a family of three.

Before we left, I took one last look at what we were leaving behind, and I knew when we walked away, our lives would never be the same. Truer words were never spoken.

CHAPTER 16

Our Charlie Brown Christmas

One day led to the next. What was before changed overnight for us. What used to be a large comfortable kitchen table with chairs in our previous home turned into a small end table I took with us to our new apartment. There were no chairs. We used pillows for chairs. I had spent all my paycheck to get us into that apartment, and I made all our meals stretch as far as possible. It was difficult to say the least, both physically and emotionally. Spiritually, the Lord kept giving me strength to move ahead with my children and leave the past behind. We all three slept in one bed, but we were warm.

One day near Christmas, my kids borrowed the car to go somewhere. When they came home, I took the car and left to go grocery shopping. They stayed in the apartment. What would happen next will forever be cherished in my heart and mind. I've relived that scene over the years, and it never ceases to bring me to tears of gratitude and love for the precious children God gifted me with.

It was really dark when I got back home. I walked in and saw this poor little Christmas tree, missing branches and all lopsided, standing in our living room. It had three socks hanging from it that had designs on them made with permanent markers, no lights, just a little Charlie Brown Christmas tree. But in this mother's heart, it was the most beautiful, magnificent, hand-decorated tree I'd ever seen. My kids had gone in search of a free Christmas tree. They were called Charlie Brown Christmas trees, the ones no one wanted. On

Christmas Eve, they were given away for free. When I walked in, my kids yelled, "Surprise, Mom!" I melted into the floor.

I could only afford one present each for them that year. But they were the most grateful kids any mother could ever be blessed with. No Christmas before or after has ever meant more to me than that night before Christmas, when my children gave me the greatest gift of all—their love.

After our divorce and with God's help, we had made a life for ourselves. God had provided an apartment for us to live in, food on the table, clothes on our back, and shoes on our feet. It wasn't easy. We went through many valleys of tough emotional and financial times as a family of three. It took three years of tightening our belts, but God made it possible for me to buy a home for us. We belonged to a wonderful church family and sat under solid foundational teaching from the Word of God.

My daughter got married, and I was there to see it! Our lives had started to heal regarding her father, and he walked her down the aisle. I was able to support my son in all of his athletics and see him graduate high school, then on to college. Never underestimate the power of God to transform lives. When we surrender our lives to Him, all things are made new.

CHAPTER 17

Change My Heart, O God... Make It Ever New

It was almost four years after our divorce. I was sitting in church, and our pastor began sharing about this lady he knew. He said that he had been at her home the night before because she had called him needing help. He told us that at one time, she had attended our church but had walked away, and he hadn't seen or heard from her in years. She had called him to tell him that her father had passed away, and she needed help. He asked us to remember her in prayer because she was at a crossroads in her walk with the Lord. He told us her name, and if I hadn't been sitting, I would have fallen flat on the floor.

It was one of the women my husband had had an affair with. She was the one that my husband was with on that fateful morning four years earlier. My heart began racing, and I felt a hot rush come over me. He went on to explain how she was a broken woman and was really hurting. Memories, memories, memories came flooding into my mind. My throat seized up, and I felt dizzy. My heart was pounding so fast I couldn't breathe. Add to that, that "voice" started talking to me again! I heard, "Go to her. Get up, and go to her." But this time, I didn't say, "You talkin' to *me*?" This time, I said, "Yes, Lord."

I turned to my sister in the Lord sitting next to me and told her what that small still voice had said to me, and without hesitation, she said, "Obey Him." She said she would pray for me, and I got up and left right in the middle of pastor talking.

When I got outside, I realized that I didn't have a car! I had ridden my bike to church since I lived just a few blocks away. And for an instant in time, a thought darted through my mind. "What are you doing?" flashed in like lightning.

And the battle was *on*! I recognized it this time. I knew what was at work this time. I put on my spiritual armor, got on that bike, and started riding toward her house, which was clear across the other side of town.

I headed to her house, praying in the wind, praying that God would direct me, give me the words, help me face the fear of rejection from her. I started crying, remembering the pain she and my husband had caused me and my children years ago. I prayed even harder because I knew those thoughts, those painful memories were coming from the discourager, the deceiver, the father of lies.

He was telling me that I couldn't ride that far and make it across town.

He was telling me that she was going to slam the door in my face, going to laugh at me, and shame me for daring to come to her door.

Through my tears, I felt something well up inside me—a strength, a boldness, a tenacity of purpose shooting through my veins. My grandmother's teachings came bursting into my memory. She had told me how to rebuke the devil, how to bind him in the name of Jesus! And I found myself speaking the Word of God's truth against the darts of the enemy assailing my mind.

I found myself pleading the blood of Jesus over me, taking authority over the lies of Satan, casting him and his minions back to the pit of hell, and reminding him of God's almighty written Word!

Then it happened. I began worshipping the Lord, singing songs of praise, and feeling a renewed strength in my legs. In God's strength, nothing was going to stop me. God is ever faithful. He is our strong tower in times of trouble. Over and over in His Word, we see His promises for us. "Do not be afraid—I am with you! I am your God—let nothing terrify you! I will make you strong and help you; I will protect you and save you" (Isaiah 41:10 GNT).

When God is by our side, He enables us to do what seems impossible for us but never impossible for Him. "I can do all things [which He has called me to do] through Him who strengthens and empowers me [to fulfill His purpose—I am self-sufficient in Christ's sufficiency; I am ready for anything and equal to anything through Him who infuses me with inner strength and confident peace]" (Philippians 4:13 AMP).

I finally made it to her house. Praying all the way, I walked up to her door and knocked. I waited for whatever was to come—no answer. I rang the doorbell—no answer.

Her neighbor next door was mowing the lawn and stopped to come over to me. She told me that she wasn't home, that she was at the funeral home making arrangements for her father who had passed away. I wanted to cry. Could I have been that wrong about all of this? I was going to walk away, but that boldness came back like a flood. I told her neighbor that I would like to leave her a note but didn't have anything to write with. She told me she would get a pencil and paper for me. After she left, I asked God to give me the words and to make them His, not mine. I said so many things in that note, things that I knew I would never be able to say to her in person.

I told her that I had hated her for a long time, but God had healed me of that kind of cancer in my heart. I asked her to forgive me. And I told her to call me if she would like to talk.

I got back on my bike and left. That was the lesson in true forgiveness God had planned for me many years before.

Life is what happens when you have other plans, and especially when you "think" you're in control.

She did call me later that evening. We talked for a long, long time. God turned what the enemy meant for evil into a manifest testament of His glorious, transforming power to change and heal broken hearts.

We ended up attending church together and renewed our friendship that was now a Christian one.

EVIE G.

Do you want to know how wonderful God's plans are for those who love Him, trust Him, and obey Him? "And I know that God will work all things together for good to those who love Him and are called according to His purpose" (Romans 8:28 NIV).

She ended up getting married (not to my ex-husband), and she asked me to sing at her wedding!

My friend died three years later from cancer.

CHAPTER 18

God Never Wastes a Hurt

In my twenty-six years as an elementary school teacher, there were times when children came from abusive backgrounds who would pass through my classroom. They were with me for nine months of their lives. I understood them, their perspectives and attitudes about life. Some had no idea that the abuse they were experiencing wasn't "normal" or that there was any other way of living.

Even in instances when I would intervene for them through child protection services, some children, more often than not, would suffer separation anxiety from their abusive parent(s).

As a child, in the midst of similar abuses going on in my family, I knew the gamut of emotions between love, hate, and confusion. My background experiences brought a deeper dimension in relating to my students; and I became a child advocate with a mission to be part of the solution for abused children and women.

The stigma of abuse perpetuates itself. Closet secrets stay hidden away. Many of us function in society with one foot in the closet and the other out.

I can't help but believe that when God breathed life into me, He must have mingled a little extra strength and hope in my soul to carry me through the trials and devastations I would face.

My life as a child wasn't always catastrophic, however. There were times sprinkled along my path when I could escape into childhood fun at family or public gatherings. There was school, friends, and teachers who cared for me and treated me with love and respect. They made me feel validated and valued as a person. I can thank God for the "sprinkling." Sometimes I found myself wishing that I could go home with some of my teachers instead of going home.

It felt as if my life was one great big roller-coaster ride of fear mixed with joy. I never knew if my home life was going to be a happy one or a fearful, raging one from one day to the next.

As a Christian and a teacher (in retrospect), I took the lessons of these adversities and, having overcome them, into the classroom with me. They served to deepen my relationships with hurting children that came to me each year. Before I became a teacher, I purposed in my heart that my classroom would be a place of refuge for all those children like me who were living in the kind of environment I grew up in. My love for hurting children and women, and what God allowed me to experience in those abusive years of my life, were never a waste. God used it all for His purposes for my life and in the lives of those who would come into my future.

CHAPTER 19

Visions I Will Never Forget

As I look back at the events that happened during my childhood, certain ones are indelibly etched in my memory. One of the most foretelling and spiritually significant ones was when we joined my aunt and her family one summer day.

We all went to the local watering hole for a day of swimming and picnicking along the riverbank.

That was the day I drowned.

Do you believe in miracles? Do you believe that Jesus died and, on the third day, rose from the dead? Do you believe that *all* things are possible with God, and for Him nothing—but nothing—is impossible? Selah.

It was a life altering event that permeated my soul. It would have a profound and lasting impact on me later in my life. The Lord would use that event as a testimony of His power and for His glory. What happened to me would later reveal the hand of God manifesting itself upon my life. But I wouldn't be aware of it until many years later. God's timing is always perfect.

The swimming hole was in a river that flowed beneath a bridge on the outskirts of town. It had wide banks on either side, shade, and was a great place to cool off during the summer. The river wasn't very wide, but it was deep. I was wading in the deep part watching my brothers and boy cousins swinging off a rope suspended from the branch of a huge tree on one side of the river. They would swing off into the air and yell like Tarzan as they let go of the rope and dive bomb into the water as close to me as they could. I was the sister and girl cousin target they tried to splash as much as possible when they hit the water.

One of my older cousins who didn't know how to swim yelled at me from the bank where he was standing nearby the tree with the rope. He kept asking me to take him to the opposite bank across the river. I was around eight or nine years old but a good swimmer. So I decided to do it. Everything was going fine as I floated him on his back across the river. But when we reached the middle of the river, he panicked. In an instant, he flipped over and started "climbing" me.

I tried to gain control of him, but before I knew it, his feet were on my shoulders, and I was fighting for my life several feet below him. The more I tried to push him off me, the tighter his feet choked my neck.

I could hear his screams above the water and see some light, but all too soon, there was nothing but blackness all around me, and I couldn't move anymore. All my strength was gone. I remember realizing that I didn't feel any pain. It was strange.

The next thing I remember was being enveloped in a mist. I was surrounded by beautiful white billowy clouds, and I was walking in them! I wondered if I was in heaven. Was this the place I heard people talk about when we used to go to church? Then I heard a voice. It was a soothing voice. I felt so at peace.

He called me His child and said that it wasn't my time yet, that He had a work for me to do.

I didn't want to leave that place and go back where I had been. I asked Him to let me stay. He told me to look. I turned to see the clouds opening up and saw my family in chaos on the bank of the river. Then with that same gentle and compassionate voice, He told me to look at what I would leave behind.

Suddenly I saw myself lying on the bank of the river, and I was dead in my mother's arms.

My mother was screaming, rocking me in her arms and inconsolable. I saw her face. I felt my mother's heart bursting in anguish. Then he told me, "This is what you'll leave behind." At that moment,

I told Him that I couldn't do that to my mother and that I wanted to go back!

Instantly I felt the water all around me once again. All I could see was blackness. Then I felt something grab my feet below me, but I wasn't afraid. The only way I can describe what happened next is that I felt my body being thrust upward like a speeding bullet.

I could feel my long hair sweeping behind my head. I couldn't move my arms as they were fixed to my side. Soon I saw light above me. It seemed so far away, but I knew, without doubt or fear, I would make it to the surface.

Then God showed me the two angels holding my feet as they rocketed me to the light up above. They had huge wings, and they glowed with the most beautiful light all around them. I saw their eyes full of love for me. I couldn't take my eyes off them! They were the most wondrous beings I had ever seen.

Just before my body broke the surface of the water, I felt my arms released from my sides and spread open like wings. I made one swooping stroke upward and reached the air, taking the deepest breath I had ever taken in my whole young life.

As I floated on my back, I didn't have the strength to swim. I couldn't speak. I couldn't move to help myself. All I could do was breathe in and float. Tears streamed down my face, becoming one with the river. I tried to regain my senses and figure out what to do. I couldn't quite understand it all, but I knew God had sent me back.

He said that He had a work for me to do, but He never told me what it was.

Questions drifted into my mind. What did it all mean? What just happened?

As I floated, unable to move, I could hear my family on the now distant bank, hovering around my cousin and still in the chaos of having saved him from drowning. But I could do nothing to let them know I was there. I was there and needed help! My strength was spent. So I continued to float, trying to regain enough strength to swim back to the bank of the river where they were.

Soon, however, I realized my body was being swept by the river downstream toward the rapids. I remember looking sideways toward the bridge ahead. I knew that it would be the turning point for me. If I didn't try to swim before I floated under that bridge, the rapids would take me. Between the flood of my tears in the river and maintaining my composure, I floated further and further downstream.

I started praying. I asked God to give me strength and the courage to swim before I got swept into the rapids ahead. I told myself that it was now or never. I pleaded, "Please help me, God!"

I flipped over and started swimming for my life. By the time I got close enough for my family to hear me, I only had strength enough to dog-paddle. When I got within ear's reach, I heard my mom yelling, "Evie! Where's Evie?" When I heard her voice and saw her face in my mind's eye, I remembered what God had shown me lying dead in her arms.

I heard myself yelling, screaming, as I made my way to her. I screamed one last time, "Help me!" And they swam out to me and carried me out of the water.

They laid me on the sand. I was in my mother's arms, and we were both crying, but I was alive and in her loving arms.

After all the emotion and trauma had settled down and before I could tell the story of what had happened, a fury came over me, and I broke away from my mother's arms.

The next thing I knew, I was on top of my cousin choking him and banging his head on the sand. He was trying to say he was sorry, but all I could see was *red*! After they pulled me off him, I shook like a leaf and sank down in a puddle of tears.

I never told anyone about my experience with God. I kept it to myself for years. The memory was to surface once again, however, but in God's timing, not mine.

Sometimes God allows us to drown in our own sins to teach us how to rise to the surface in His and only His power.

And sometimes He uses the seemingly unbelievable to thrust us from the depths of doubt to the reality and light of His truth.

God's truth is the standard by which all other truth is measured. We have choices.

We can choose to believe in God's truth, about His existence, and HIStory given to us by His inspired word or not. We can choose to believe in other world views of spontaneous evolution without God as well. However, John 8:32 (GNT) tells us, "You will know the truth, and the truth will set you free."

Free from doubt, free from fear, free from the lies of the enemy of our soul, free to understand the one and only truth found in God's Word—it's our choice. I made mine. My heart, mind, emotions, hope, and life were made brand-new, and what He's done for me, He is ready, waiting, and so willing to do for you.

CHAPTER 20

What's the "Matter" All About?

Choices—life is filled with choices we all must make. My mind goes back to what I learned in science about matter. Science teaches that there are three states of matter: solid, liquid, and gas. I contend there is one more, namely, plasma. It's the "stuff" floating around that is unseen in the air and atmosphere surrounding us. It's the matter that cannot be destroyed. Here on earth and in the cosmos, I believe there is what I call *plasmotic matter*. Many maintain all that exists in our known world and even in our unknown world as coming into existence from a Big Bang in the cosmos, which then led to our planet, which then led to spontaneous life emerging from primordial soup.

Before I became a Christian, questions I asked myself about all these theories and beliefs were a trek of inquiry and exploration for me. What was true about our being? Which of the many, many beliefs were true for me? Choices…

After I became a Christian and a teacher by profession, teaching in the public school system was a challenge for me in the areas of science and history. Before I was a follower of Christ, I was exposed to the theory of evolution in school. In addition to my role as a teacher, I became a science staff developer, traveling with a cadre of other staff developers, throughout the state of California. Science was a subject of awe and wonder to me. But I always took issue with teaching the component of science as it related to the subject of evolution. Regardless of that, I remember how excited I always was when I had to teach the theory of evolution in my classroom. As I presented it, God gave me so many opportunities to share the fundamental values and beliefs held by others who believe in divine creation. It wasn't in the science books I taught from. But I was compelled within me to equitably present the belief in divine creation to my students as well. New age beliefs and indoctrination of those beliefs had been creeping into the California state adopted curriculum for some time in my career.

When I was an elementary student, divine creation was always a theory presented along with other theories about the creation narrative. It was part of the curriculum. By the time I became a teacher, all that had changed. God was taken out of the curriculum. He was replaced with studies in New Age, Eastern religion, and every religious belief system, except that of divine creation. We were to teach "tolerance" of diversity in beliefs. But the only belief that was not "tolerated" in the teaching of diverse beliefs was Christianity.

I knew in my heart that God had placed me in a position to make learning the *truth* as I knew it, and God gave it, part of my calling in the public school system.

We weren't supposed to teach about the Christian belief, but I never let that stop me. When it came to teaching world history, the story was the same. The curriculum had morphed into biased, antipatriotic, and skewed anti-establishment views of America's history. As a dedicated professional, I taught the curriculum that I was given to teach. It thrilled me when including the Christian perspective, it generated many questions from my students about opposing beliefs. The discussions were awesome. My conviction to educate my students beyond the myopic, federally mandated curriculum of secular science and historical information was immovable.

Over the years, I observed many changes in the kind of curricular content being adopted in our science and history books. The NEA (National Education Association) was adopting and promoting the phasing out of the fundamental Christian values and beliefs of our founding fathers. It became more and more evident in the curriculum being adopted.

What once were history books containing our ideals of democracy, freedom, honor for our flag and respect for America began shifting to the left. Love of country became hate curriculum devised to enculturate a new mindset in our youth. Under the guise of so-called "tolerance" for the rainbow of differing values and beliefs, the only values that were not included were the foundational beliefs upon which America was rooted and founded by our founding fathers.

It was larcenous. Its slow, incremental implementation reminded me of the "frog" analogy.

A frog was put in a pot of cold water and placed on a stove. Ever so slowly, the heat was incrementally raised so that the frog became accustomed to the rising temperature. It stayed there, unaware of the impending danger, until it finally boiled to death without a fight.

That's how Satan works. His attacks are done with covert actions in the unseen realm. He distracts the minds of unsuspecting, unaware, and secularly indoctrinated lives. We become oblivious to the rising temperature that takes us to fiery, eternal damnation. He lulls the hearts, minds, and souls of mankind incrementally into the flames of hell for eternity.

As Billy Graham so wisely put it, "Don't think of Satan as a harmless cartoon character with a red suit and a pitchfork. He is very clever and powerful, and his unchanging purpose is to defeat God's plan at every turn, including his plan for your life."

I witnessed the curricular inoculation of socialistic ideology injected into and slowly replacing our traditional American values. And those antifundamental beliefs were specifically targeted at our youth, the future leaders of America, to lull them into adopting a belief that government (not the people) should rule our society. Choices—God's way or man's way.

I did all I could to share the love of country, speak to, and defend the truth that our country was established on. The Lord gave me young charges every year that I was thankful for and was privileged to teach. I'll be forever thankful for the opportunity to have shared the love of Christ and the truth of God in my classroom every day. What defined me wasn't being a teacher. Being a Christian, whose profession was that of teaching, was what defined me. My students had the right to hear and learn about the truth regarding Christian beliefs as well as the other beliefs that were infiltrated into their curriculum. My convictions and beliefs lived deep within me, and I was obligated by them to widen the knowledge base of my students in their studies across the spectrum of education. God wouldn't have it any other way, nor would I.

CHAPTER 21

He Will Give You the Desires of Your Heart

Do you recall when I spoke of some family members who had an abiding relationship with God, those tumultuous years when I trusted no one and was a doubting Thomas about everything?

On my mom's side of the family, I had five uncles and one aunt. One of mom's brothers was a minister. Some were followers of Christ, the ones I referred to as being "different." God showed me glimpses into their lives. They talked about the healing power of Jesus and of miracles they had seen. But to me, they were just stories, conversations during their visits. The day came, however, that God would open my eyes and grant me one of the desires of my heart involving these family members.

It was a few years after I became a Christian that He would answer a specific prayer of mine. It was a deep desire that I had wanted for a long time. I remembered hearing my mom's family talking about the healing power and miracles of God. I longed to see those so very much. It wasn't because I doubted in God's power. I knew that I knew that I knew that nothing was impossible for Him. But I wanted to know why the faces of my uncles and aunts glowed, and they cried with such fervor when talking about their experiences in seeing God's healings and miracles.

MY BROKEN PIECES—HIS YIELDED CLAY

It was under bittersweet circumstances that God manifested His healing, miraculous power to me and indeed answered my prayer.

Once again, I would see the truth of God's Word with my own eyes. I would see how real His Word is that promises to "give us the desires of our heart" (Psalm 37:4 NIV).

It happened when one of my mother's brothers, who was in the hospital, was given a very short time to live. The family was called in. All of us packed into his hospital room, and we were standing wall to wall in his room. Because of diabetes, he had been blind for several years.

As we leaned down close to him, we each told him who we were and how much we loved him. One of my uncles led us in prayer. Within minutes, people started praising God, speaking in tongues, and I could feel the presence of the Holy Spirit fill the room.

I opened my eyes because I heard my uncle crying and speaking in tongues from his hospital bed. His hands were raised, and he had such a glow of joy all over his face. The presence of the Holy Spirit was overwhelming and wonderful. Then slowly, we became quiet and still. We saw my uncle open his eyes, and he was looking around the room. He "saw" my sister's son standing there and named him. Then he started saying hello to others standing around the room, naming them one by one! Someone said, "He can see!"

I can't tell you what rapture, what joy, what ecstasy filled that room! People were crying, jumping up and down, hugging him, and praising God like I'd never seen before. My uncle was touching faces, crying, praising the Lord, and thanking Him for his sight. My cousin, his daughter, was standing next to me, sobbing tears of joy along with me. Then I heard a sweet, gentle voice say, "Tell her it's my gift to her." I turned and whispered it to her, telling her that God had told me to tell her that. Her knees buckled, and I caught her as she was so overcome with joy and gratitude for what God had done.

There was so much celebration going on that a nurse bolted into the room and told us to leave. She immediately looked at his monitors that were going wild and ordered us out of the room!

We left happy, crying, thanking the Lord, and congregated out in the family waiting room. They didn't let anyone but his children and his wife back in the room.

My uncle died three hours later. I held my mom in my arms, and we cried bittersweet tears.

Sometimes there are people who can see the physical but are blind to the spiritual. And sometimes there are people who are blind but see.

There are those who don't believe in God. But that doesn't change the fact that He exists. There are some who believe in God, but they don't believe He still performs miracles. And finally, there are people who don't believe that God is still on the throne and still heals today.

I'm not one of them. Praise God!

I believe in the power of prayer. I believe God hears and answers us. Sometimes it's yes. Sometimes it's no. And sometimes it's wait.

In the KJV definition, the word *wait* means "to stay or rest in expectation and patience." In Psalm 25 and Proverbs 20, it means "to be ready to serve; to obey."

As a Christian, one of the most difficult but invaluable lessons I learned was the importance of waiting on the Lord and having patience with trusting expectation. At one time, my idea of waiting used to be praying harder, louder, longer, and over and over again until I was sure God heard me. I didn't know any better. I thought that was how getting prayers answered worked, like the kid who asks and asks and asks his daddy for something over and again until he finally gets what he wants. That's how I thought prayers and petitions were supposed to be done. I thought that to "pray unceasingly" meant to pray over and over for that which you are praying for. I misinterpreted 1 Thessalonians 5:17 (KJV): "Pray without ceasing." Praying without ceasing means being in a devotional frame of mind in the daily circumstances of our lives.

We are to have an attitude of God-consciousness, an awareness that God is always with us in our thoughts and actions. And when we ask in prayer, we need to ask, believing that God hears us and that he answers prayers.

We see many scriptures that tell us God hears and answers our prayers. "If you have faith when you pray, you will be given whatever you ask for" (Matthew 21:22 CEV).

"He hears us whenever we ask him; and since we know this is true, we know also that He gives us what we ask from Him" (1 John 5:15 GNT).

I learned that prayer is the key to heaven. But faith unlocks the door. And faith in its truest sense is not based on the amount of faith (in God) we have. The size of our faith doesn't matter as evidenced by the scripture in which Jesus said, "For truly I tell you, if you have faith the size of a mustard seed, you can say to this mountain, 'Move from here to there,' and it will move. Nothing will be impossible for you" (Matthew 17:20).

When our faith (even as small as a mustard seed) is placed in the omnipotent hands of God, nothing is impossible and amazing, wonderous, unbelievable things can happen.

CHAPTER 22

God Heard Me the First Time

One day I was talking to a dear old friend about my children, grandchildren, and loved ones. I shared my heart's deepest desire to someday see all my unsaved loved ones come to the Lord. I told him how I pleaded with God through heartfelt tears all the time for their salvation. He asked me if I trusted the Lord. He asked me if I believed that He hears and answers prayers. I answered yes to all of that. Then this wise old Christian friend of mine told me something that would forever resonate with me and change the way I thought about prayer and petitions. He said, "Sister Evie, you have to ask in prayer, trusting, and in faith, believing that God heard you the first time."

He went on to add, "After that, just start thanking Him for the answers (whatever they may be) and surrender them to His perfect will." Wow. I hadn't thought of it that way. God heard me the first time. How could I not realize that? So that's what I started doing. I gave them over to God. I started releasing the heaviness in my heart that I was carrying for my unsaved loved ones and all other prayers and petitions I would take to the Lord. And that sense of peace in my soul replaced the desperate unrest that always beset me about the salvation of my loved ones. My prayers and requests became an act of trust, belief, faith, and surrender to the omnipotent, loving Father in heaven, for whom nothing is impossible.

God tells us in His Word that we are not burden bearers. "Come to me all you who are struggling hard and carrying heavy loads, and

MY BROKEN PIECES—HIS YIELDED CLAY

I will give you rest. Put on my yoke and learn from me. I'm gentle and humble. And you will find rest for yourselves. My yoke is easy to bear, and my burden is light" (Matthew 11:28–30 CEB).

I gave my loved ones and my heartfelt prayers back to the Lord. I released their lives and my petitions into His hands. I stopped trying to "help Him" make a decision regarding them. I simply thanked Him with all my soul for what He'd done, what He was doing, and for what He had yet to do in every condition and circumstance I asked about.

When it comes to salvation, I can't make the choice for others. No one can. My grandmother prayed for me. And in God's perfect timing, not hers, I made the choice to come to Jesus.

He heard her the first time.

The cross and Christ crucified must be the object of our faith. I had to learn that faith in the finished work of Jesus at calvary is the source of all our needs being met. Because of His sacrifice, we can now go boldly before the throne of God and ask anything in Jesus' name and know that God not only hears our prayers but answers them as well. All the answers of man are found at the foot of the cross.

At the cross, we can find all the answers. There is

- forgiveness of sins (past, present, future),
- mercy (compassion for us),
- hope (joy unspeakable),
- grace (unmerited favor),
- promise of eternal life (for all who choose),
- peace (that surpasses all understanding),
- redemption (our salvation paid for by Jesus at the cross),
- strength (through the Holy Spirit of God),
- direction and guidance (from God, our light),
- healing (from God, the great physician),
- restoration (by God's power to renew us),
- provision (by God's abundance),
- wisdom (from God),
- power (given to us by Jesus's shed blood on the cross),

- ➢ love (of God and for others),
- ➢ purpose (for those who love God and are called according to His purpose),
- ➢ transformation (of our heart and character),
- ➢ sanctification (progressive transformation of our lives),
- ➢ justification (made righteous through Christ),
- ➢ knowledge (of HIStory),
- ➢ understanding (of God's Word written on our hearts),
- ➢ worship, adoration, humble and contrite spirit, gratefulness, praise (toward Jesus and the sacrifice of His shed blood for all of us).

All glory, all honor, all praise, all thanksgiving, all power be unto God! He is faithful and just, and His mercies are new every morning! "The steadfast love of the Lord never ceases; His mercies never come to an end; they are new every morning; great is Your faithfulness" (Lamentations 3:22–23 ESV).

CHAPTER 23

Bang! Went the Little Spinning Gray Cells in My Head

After becoming a Christian, I remember how, as a child, I was always searching for answers and how that same kind of hunger became even more pronounced for the things and knowledge of God. While God was teaching me, He took me back to the beginning of His inspired Word. I read Genesis 1:1–2, and I couldn't move past that. He stopped me right there. As I lingered there, pondering those words, I read that passage over again. Questions and revelations began to swirl around in my mind. My mom always told me, "*Con hablando, se entiende todo,*" which means, "Communication is the pathway to understanding." Well God surely began to communicate with me through His Holy Word. And I started to understand the significance of His not letting me move forward in my reading until He revealed His truth to me in depth in those few beginning sentences.

I read, "In the beginning, God created the heavens and the earth." Stop right there. It didn't say, "In the beginning, the *big bang* created the heavens and the earth." Now if God said it, I believe it, and that settles it for me.

The passage goes on to say, "Now the earth was formless and empty, darkness was over the surface of the deep, and the Spirit of God was hovering over the waters." Stop right there again.

Earth had no form yet. In the creation narrative, it was an incoherent waste of emptiness, a formless, lifeless, uninhabited, chaotic mass of elements, matter, unformed and void. It was an abyss of water enveloped in darkness, a surging mass of shapeless matter. But then the Spirit of God hovered over it and brought the chaotic mix of matter into order.

He then took what was there and created all that we know as life and the cosmos, seen and unseen. Who could have done such a thing? Who but God, the Creator of all that exists from the number of molecules required to give a crystalline formation its unique structure and composition, to the number of atoms it takes to create a nuclear reaction, to the number of rotations and speed therein it takes for our earth to stay on its axis, could have done that?

Who could have created gravity and force, or the genes that are unique to each and every form of life? Who but God, our Omnipotent Father of all creation could have created such unsearchable wonder and complexity? A *big bang*? Hellooooooo! And did I mention the one-celled amoeba and the unfathomable, wonderful, and fearfully made human being?

I recall the day that God put a kind of stamp on all my questions and made it indelibly settled in my mind. It was when I asked myself the following: If those who believe in evolution and the Big Bang theory believe that all that exists was a random accident, a spontaneous reaction that led to life crawling out of primordial soup, and they really believe that existence came into being that way, then how do they account for the origin of matter? Everything, every known thing, has a source. Whether we're talking about cause and effect in our daily lives or chemical reactions that take place in nuclear fusion, all outcomes must have, do have, a "source," an "origin."

If the big bang of existence came into being that way—from something that exploded—where did the "stuff," the elements, the "matter," the "something" that composed the entity that blew up come from?

How do we account for that? Where did that "matter" come from? What was its source? Something does not come from nothing. I kept going back to the word origin. There's nothing new under the sun. Everything that exists has always been because God spoke it into being. Matter can neither be created by man nor destroyed by man. It takes what already exists as "matter" to create something. And even if man seemingly destroys matter, it's never really gone. It simply changes form and becomes part of the unseen plasma around us.

Everything that man creates must have its creator, its originator, an "origin." So does life. Life, as we know it, had to have a Creator, a source of creation. From the unformed chaotic mass of elements swirling around the cosmos to the creations of man here on earth, everything short of God had to and has to have a Creator. Simply put, a building doesn't spontaneously appear. It must first have an architect who designs it. Our Creator is the master architect of the universe.

It takes unmovable, unshakeable faith in a divine Creator to believe that. God made the book of Genesis come alive for me.

As a young girl, I remember asking a priest that I met one day a question about God. I came from a Protestant background and was curious about what Catholics believed. I asked him who created God. I was an inquisitive agitator of the status quo back then. His answer was simple but unacceptable to me at the time. He said, "God always was." I couldn't wrap my head around that. I pressed him on the question. I responded with "Well if He always existed, He had to have a Creator who created Him, and that Creator had to have a Creator who created Him too, and so on and so on, right? He just smiled and said, "God always was and there was no other before Him."

I walked away thinking he had no idea. He had no answer that could prove he was right. *Stumped him*, I thought pridefully! I didn't know about *faith*, fundamental values and beliefs back then. But my forgiving, precious, and patient heavenly Father would show me many, many years later that the priest had told me the truth.

There are mysteries that we won't know the answers to until we stand before the Lord one day in heaven. Origins, answers, will all be revealed. That's the way God has designed it. We know now only some of the answers. But someday we'll know it all as God unfolds the answers to us. Until then, faith, belief in God, and His infallible, inerrant Word is all I need. His Word reassures us of it. "For now (in this time of imperfection), we see in a mirror dimly (a blurred reflection, a riddle, an enigma) but then (when the time of perfection comes, we will see reality) face-to-face. Now I know in part (just in fragments), but then I will know fully just as I have been fully known (by God)" (1 Corinthians 13:12 AMP).

In my hunger for a deeper relationship and knowledge of God, He took me to the book of Job. I thought I had cornered the market on questions about God. After reading the story of this man Job, my questions seemed more like those of a child in comparison to the questioning that went on between Job and God.

I found myself thinking about the anatomy of an ant in comparison to that of a human. To say that there are vast differences between them would be the ultimate understatement that was ever spoken.

Each anatomy in and of itself has intricacies so minute and unfathomably well ordered that random inception and creation of them is unbelievable. Only God could have created such uniquely fashioned precision.

The ant doesn't have an anatomical heart as humans do, yet it lives and functions as a living creation. What keeps it alive? Who of us could have created it? Did we have a plan for its creation?

Can we answer why there is a nucleus in a living cell? Why is the length of a day twenty-four hours and not thirty or eleven on our planet in relation to the other planets? Do we have the wisdom to know to calculate why it's ordered that way?

The DNA code of our genetic makeup is three billion letters long! And that's the DNA information in just *one* cell!

Our wisdom, knowledge, and answers about Creation are comparable to the expanse in knowledge between an ant and mankind.

How can we even begin to contemplate that we have all the answers when it comes to having the understanding of God and His unspeakable, unsearchable, magnificent creation?

Bang! The little spinning gray cells in my brain were blown out of orbit to which my daughter would say, "There goes Mom with her visuals!"

CHAPTER 24

God Turns Weeping into Joy in the Morning

Another "valley" experience entered into my life regarding my mom. When she was ninety-three years old, she began exhibiting symptoms of Alzheimer's. By the age of ninety-five, her health was declining rapidly as the Alzheimer's progressed. She had her first stroke in 2016. I moved in with her so we could care for her. Six months later, she had a second stroke.

At the hospital, her doctors told us that we needed to start discussing hospice for her. I didn't really know what that all meant at the time. But it was explained to us that her body was declining and that she was given one to six months to live. They couldn't do anymore for her and asked us what we wanted to do. Without hesitation, we took her home to care for her remaining days in her own home. Hospice came and were indeed a godsend to all of us. Mom passed away peacefully with loved ones by her side months later in 2018.

Those were heart-wrenching days. Each day had brought new health issues for Mom. She went from being a vibrant, joyous person who loved life and all her loved ones to a person whose life became totally, completely dependent on us for all her needs. It was heartbreaking to see her decline. We experienced joyous laughter some days. And there were days that the grip and thought of losing her was too much to bear. When she could no longer walk, she was devastated. When she could no longer move without help, it broke our hearts. There were nights without end because of her Alzheimer's when she couldn't sleep. It saddened us to the core when we had to start using a Hoyer to lift her out of bed several times a day and saw the look of sadness in her eyes. But God helped us to be strong for her and say or do something that would make all of us laugh, and it would take the sting out of the pain of seeing her in that condition.

At night when it was my brother's turn to listen for her voice in case she called out, I would go to her den where I slept and pour my heart out to God.

There were four dear loved ones who died within those two years of Mom's illness. They were all on Mom's side of the family. We didn't tell her. We wanted to protect her. I found myself spending more and more time writing my feelings down as a way of release. I gave them to God and asked Him to help me, to help us all to take care of Mom and make her days as beautiful and as happy as possible.

One night I wrote a prayer: *Father, in the midst of joy, You are there. In the midst of the storm, You are there. You are the arms of strength and love, of peace and comfort. You are our words when we can't find the strength to speak. You are the One who bottles every tear and wastes not one single hurt. When we are weak, You tell us to give our weaknesses to You because You are strong and can carry all our burdens for us. When life overwhelms us with pain, sorrow, and confusion, You send Your comforter to touch our mind, our soul, our heart; and You give us Your peace that goes beyond our understanding. Your grace, Your unmerited favor, is the refuge and resolve You gift us with in our adversities. I ask You to carry us and Mom in Your loving arms. Your yoke is easy, and Your burden is light. Envelop us in Your strength, Your comfort, Your peace, Your wisdom, Your courage, and Your healing touch. I lift my mom up to You with thanksgiving and praise in my heart. Meet each and every need she has. Thank You, Father, for all You are doing for us now and will do in the days to come. I plead the blood of Jesus over Mom and all of us who love her and are caring for her. May Thy will be done, Father. I know that You will work all things together for the good of those who love You and are called according to Your purpose. Bless my mom, dear Lord. Thank You that we can trust You at all times and in every circumstance even when it's difficult, especially when it's difficult, but not for You. I thank You for answering prayers and for Your faithfulness. I ask You and thank You in all these things in Jesus' name. Amen.*

I thank God for the days of laughter we had with Mom. I thank Him for the meals at the table, even if she was in a wheelchair, when she and I would sing our hearts out praising Jesus. I even thank God for the tears she and I shed together, sometimes tears of sheer joy and sometimes tears of sorrow. But we thanked God together for all of it—happy, sad—it didn't matter to us. We celebrated each and every moment together, even when she sometimes forgot who I was or where she was. God gave us both the grace to see it all through. Even when Mom could no longer sing, it was those worship songs we used to sing together that would bring a smile to her face and joy to her heart. I thank God for every moment of every day He gave us with her in her last days and precious years. They were a gift from our merciful God.

Now here I am, two years after Mom went home to be with the Lord. It's November 2020. It has passed so quickly. I learned so much more about God's faithfulness, love, and mercy during that time with Mom. If I had it to do all over again, oh, how I would. My solace is that I *know* one day I'll see my beautiful, precious mother again in heaven, and, oh, what a day of rejoicing that will be!

CHAPTER 25

Dear Lord, I Need An MRI!

That valley experience was so very difficult for Mom and all of us who took care of her. But even more so was the year after she died.

The first year after Mom's passing, I experienced a continuing roller-coaster ride of emotions. There were many "firsts" without her. She passed away the month before Christmas. And eighteen months later, my oldest brother, who was my best friend, passed away. More "firsts" would come.

When Mom was healthy in years past, I would sometimes call her up before I left on one of my trips to my grandson's wrestling tournaments up north. The month after she died, I went on one of those trips to see him wrestle. I was, as always, thrilled to go visit my son (his wrestling coach) and my daughter-in-law to join them at their tournaments. I was running back and forth with the team from one gym to the next, following my grandson's matches. It was good to get away for a while and distract my mind from all the legalities and arrangements of Mom's estate. Add to that the pain in my heart, having to make and coordinate all the difficult decisions she had entrusted us with. It was a kind of respite for me to be away from it all for a while.

There was a surreal moment in time when I was sitting in a chair by the wrestling mat where my grandson had just finished his match. Suddenly, even though the room was full of people, I felt all alone. My mind drifted to Mom's bed the moment she passed away in front of me. As I sat there, tears started pouring down my face. and I couldn't shake the pain. It seemed like I was there in her bedroom all over again. I guess my son saw it happening to me because the next thing I could feel was his hand on my shoulder asking me if I was okay. He knew what was happening to me. I could see it in his face. Looking into his eyes, I got back up and walked off the gym floor with him. Another "first" in the many to come.

Some days I would wake up and go about my business and not feel so sad. Then there were those days when I would think about calling Mom to talk to her, and it would hit me like a tsunami that she wasn't here to talk to. Those days were hard to recover from.

I knew those days would happen in mourning my mom. I knew it in my head, but my heart didn't feel better knowing that. Knowing that didn't help ease the pain of not being able to kiss Mom or sing with her, hug her, or laugh with her. I couldn't even cry with her anymore. I couldn't get up in the morning, go to her room to get her ready for her day. I couldn't walk in like I always did and greet her with "Good morning, sunshine!" and see her smile and say it back to me. That first year was like being in a haze in so many ways. My saving grace was always talking to God about it all.

One very difficult day of missing her, I sat myself down and took my depression and pain to the Lord. How could I shake these feelings, get past them, and try instead to remember that she was in glory, standing whole, and healed? That quiet time I spent with the Lord took me to a scripture. I found such peace after reading it. It was in the book of Psalms. "When the righteous cry for help, the Lord hears and delivers them out of all their troubles. The Lord is near to the brokenhearted and saves the crushed in spirit" (Psalm 34:17–18 RSV).

I was so encouraged by that scripture that I started talking to myself, shaking free from all the negativity and toxic input I was allowing into my heart. I began writing my feelings down once again and had a good conversation with my*self*. After I finished scolding and encouraging myself, it was so very empowering and self-edifying that I felt renewed in my spirit, and I thanked the Lord for the joy He filled my soul with that day. His love is truly joy unspeakable!

The following came pouring out of me:

Consider your*self*. Have you ever talked to yourself—seriously—I mean really taken time to steal away with your*self*, sat yourself down, quieted your spirit, removed all distractions and talked to yourself? I'll call it thinking outside the little spinning gray cells. When you do this, powerful insights about who you are—really are—can impact your life dramatically.

This practice can open your eyes to see the truth about yourself in the intimate privacy between you and God alone. While some may think this to be kind of quirky (talking to yourself), others might think it a strange thing to do, and yet others even think it's time to call those little men in the funny white suits to come and take you away. Talking to yourself can expose realities about you that can change your life (not by taking you to the funny farm) but in a positive, productive way.

The sons of Korah, who some believe wrote Psalm 42:5 (GNT), give us an example of this introspect practice in the following verse: "Why am I so sad? Why am I so troubled? I will put my hope in God, and once again, I will praise Him, my Savior and my God."

It's an account of a man who was spiritually depressed.

We see a man who sits himself down and has a heart-to-heart talk with himself. He questions himself, asking why his soul is so sad and depressed. His soul (mind, will, and emotions) is perplexed. He tries to examine why his mind is flooded with despair. He tries to understand why his will to do or not do is being so adversely affected within him. And he asks himself why his emotions are so overwhelmed with this depression.

This conversation with himself leads him to a firm and resolute answer, which transcends his oppressed state of being. He resolves that in spite of this turmoil within him, he will yet seek God for his strength, joy, and hope. He will praise Him in the midst of it all.

He will, with the help of God, overcome his turmoil and look to God, the One for whom nothing is impossible for his answers.

That is our answer.

It's talking to ourselves instead of listening to the enemy of our soul, the author of confusion and father of lies, Satan. If we are to live a life of joy and hope, we need to examine our inner *self* when we are confused, depressed, fearful, and when the whole gamut of unrest is darted against us.

God is not the bestower of confusion and lies. We must recognize the source of all those things that are meant to destroy us and our relationship with Him. We must remember who we are in Christ, who God is, what He has done for us and is yet to do. We must put on the full armor of God and fight on our knees in order to overcome spiritual depression and all other attacks of the enemy—yes, even in the mourning process.

How? We appropriate the weapons of our warfare available to us. We talk to ourselves and ask God to reveal the truth about us and ask Him to strengthen, guide, protect, and to champion our inner struggles and battles *for* us. It's healthy to release tears and let it all out when we need to. But it's unhealthy for us to allow depression to take hold of our soul.

Imagine yourself under an X-ray that is focused over your heart and mind. It will reveal the physical parts like your bones, what they look like, their shape, and appearance. But put yourself under an MRI, and you're going to see the deepest tissue parts of those same bones and organs that an X-ray only touches the surface of. In the same sense, an X-ray of our *life* in the "physical" manifested realm reveals (by our actions) our heart and mind's state of being. It is evidenced by the things we do, the things that are visible manifestations, resulting from our thoughts—it's "surface" stuff that shows us in our actions.

More revealing, however, is an MRI of our spiritual life. It goes beyond the physical parts of our lives (in our heart and mind) that are known to and are only seen by God.

That, my dear friends, is what I mean when I refer to talking to your*self*. Doing so is like placing your innermost being, your spiritual essence, under an MRI of your soul before God.

Another way of looking at the letters MRI might be thinking of them as a *m*ost *r*evealing *i*ntrospection or *m*ust *r*eevaluate *i*ntrinsically.

When God helps us see the truth about ourselves, we may feel shock and awe and rather see the MRI as *m*ust *r*un *i*mmediately!

But no, being honest with ourselves—totally, completely uncovered, and transparent before God—can be the *m*ost *r*enovating *i*nsight of God's sanctification process and our progressive transformation as Christians.

During that quiet time with the Lord, I began talking to myself because I had been struggling with an ongoing battle within me. It was in that conversation (questioning, probing, examining the reasons and sources behind my struggle) that God's hand touched my eyes, heart, and mind. He opened them completely and lifted the veil of confusion; and He revealed the utter truth behind my struggle. There, undone at His feet in overwhelming gratitude for the revelation He gave me about myself, I experienced a kind of release in my spirit like never before.

Know the truth, and it shall set you free. God took me to a place where, in talking to myself and asking Him to help me understand the chains that had my will tethered, He showed me the source of my struggle.

Talking to ourselves in those quiet steal away with God moments, opens pathways to understanding more about who we are and whose we are as children of God. Therein we can find resolve, direction, and revelation. The practice of talking to ourselves before God's mirror of transparency is key to unlocking answers to the struggles and battles within us. As we do this and seek God concerning the answers, He illuminates the mirror of clarity before our eyes. We see the whole scenario of our condition.

Constant introspection of the condition of our heart and seeking the truth behind our motives become spiritual food for our soul. Ultimately, surrendering our*self* to God opens the door for the *m*aster *r*edeemer's *i*nfinite plan to unfold in our lives. There is no greater MRI than He.

CHAPTER 26

Worship the Lord Your God, and Serve Him Only

In my desire to help hurting women impacted by abuse and other life issues, I searched the Scriptures, researched publications, and drew from my own experiences of abuse so that I might one day share the journey of my victory through Christ Jesus over them. God strategically brought a couple of Christian authors' writings into my sphere of reading. They were Tony Evans, a current minister, author and pastor in Texas, along with another author who was born in 1874 named Oswald Chambers.

One of Tony's books, *Victory in Spiritual Warfare: Outfitting Yourself for the Battle*, taught me more in depth about spiritual battles in the unseen realm, which wage against our lives. One of Oswald Chamber's books, *My Utmost for His Highest*, took me on a deep dive regarding surrendering oneself to God. I was so enthralled with their insights that I created a series of teachings on spiritual warfare and on what it meant to surrender to the Lord in every facet of our lives. I embarked on this endeavor and enlisted my enthusiastic friend, Joan Constable, to help me with the classes at our church. She was and is one of those "a friend in need is a friend indeed" persons to me. God brought her into my life to co-champion the support and love that our sisters in the Lord so often need in the darkness of adversity.

In Tony's opening chapter, "The Nature of the Battle," he states, "If all you see is what you see, you will never see all that there is to be seen." In God's Word, the apostle Paul tells us that we "wrestle not against flesh and blood (humans) but against the powers and rulers in the unseen spiritual realm" (Ephesians 6:12 NIV). That's where our victories are won. That's where I learned to fight on my knees.

Of equal significance, Oswald Chambers in his book, *My Utmost for His Highest*, tells us in one of his devotional excerpts, "We will all feel very much ashamed if we do not yield to Jesus the areas of our lives. He has asked us to yield to Him…to reach that level of determination is a matter of the will, not of debate or of reasoning. It is absolute and irrevocable surrender of the will at that point."

I teach and share with others the need to surrender and abandon our will to God. Known intimately to me is the struggle and tug of war that comes with attempts to do so.

Therein lies the battle. Easier said than done, right? It's always that way when we try to go it alone without the help of God.

And yet the choices are always before us. Let go and surrender to God's will? Abandon our will, our innermost being, thinking, speaking, and actions to God? Our heart to God? Say no to our fleshly desires, the strongholds that bind us, and yes, lay them at the foot of the cross?

Tall order, challenging choices—but we must choose. This I know. We can't do it victoriously without the help of the Holy Spirit. As Christians, we are compelled by the drawing of the Holy Spirit to choose who we will serve. "If it is unacceptable in your sight to serve the Lord, choose for yourselves this day whom you will serve. But as for me and my house, we will serve the Lord" (Joshua 24:15 AMP).

From a fleshly perspective, every carnal cell in us screams in resistance to surrendering our will to God. We will all come to a crossroad one day when we either choose to please the flesh (our carnal nature) or to please God. We will choose what and whom we love the most. That's the painful reality that wars against us over choosing the love of God or the love of the world. Until we surrender that which is carnal and carries so many sinful regrets and eternal consequences, we will never know the unfathomable joy of serving the Lord who gives us the gift of unspeakable peace in our hearts and salvation for our soul.

So we come to those crossroads of the straight and narrow path that leads to the Lord or the wide path that leads to eternal separation from God. Our journey to eternal life with God has a multitude of deviant paths, all crafted by Satan, the enemy of our souls and the father of lies. They are paths that entice us to quench our lustful desires, those things that distract and lead us to the depths of indulgence and consummating our sins. But I've come to realize that there is a time and place along these crossroads when we merge to that one juncture of ultimate decision. If we choose God and we purpose in our heart to follow Him, we make the eternally rewarding choice that leads to life in the presence of God forever. Knowing that we can do nothing without Him, without His strength, His power and His leading becomes fully revealed.

I never acknowledged that fact. I functioned most of my life without serving God or realizing He was in it. It wasn't until He opened my blinded eyes that I saw the truth of my existence. He showed me that if it weren't for the breath He breathed into me, I wouldn't even be able to move my little finger. We live day-to-day thinking that we are alive and breathing, functioning in the world, and doing so just fine without God. But He *is* with us. He's in every step we take, every move we make. It's the breath of life He's given us that makes our existence possible even when we do not realize, acknowledge, or believe it.

It's then when we humbly bow the knee, acknowledge, and confess our utter need for Him and for His will to permeate our lives that surrendering to eternal rewards and a forgiven life can truly begin.

That step leads to a fully abandoned will on the path He's planned for us. That is where we come face-to-face with ourselves. As though a mirror were placed before us, the blindfolds that hindered the truth are removed. We see clearly, more transparently, than ever before. We face the reality of the unseen spiritual battleground we've been in. And we say *yes* to the Lord.

Always around the corner, the destroyer raises his ugly head, roaring and raging, waiting to rip our eyes away from God's truth.

He tries to slither his way into our thoughts and drip his toxic lies into our mind and into our heart. But we have an advocate! We have a host of angels! We have the strength and power of Almighty God on our side! We stand on the Word of God, the sword of the Spirit, who battles for us! We put on the whole armor of God, appropriate its power, and walk victoriously against our enemies! We claim God's Word! "No weapon that is formed against you will succeed" (Isaiah 54:17 AMP). We have the protection of God on our side. "So do not fear, for I am with you; do not be dismayed, for I am your God. I will strengthen you and help you; I will uphold you with my righteous right hand" (Isaiah 41:10 CSB).

We make the choice, and in doing so, our weaknesses are replaced with the power of our omnipotent Father.

Our desire to do God's will, to become His will, overrides all else. We yearn to become undone in complete abandon, total surrender, and let God sever the willful chains that bind us. There, at the crossroads of surrender and abandon, our will becomes one with God's will. The Potter can then truly use His clay. The Master Weaver can then truly weave the tapestry of our lives to create His masterpiece, His perfect purpose, and divine design for us. We follow the straight and narrow path. And we cling tenaciously to the hem of His garment all the way, one moment, one step, one day at a time.

In God's sovereign plan for me, from my youth until present day, He has taken me on a journey of His own making. He knew me before I was knitted in my mother's womb. He knew that it would take me years to write this book. There were many lesson, valleys, and introspective events that would need to occur in my life before He revealed it was time—time to finish this book—His book, HIStory and MYstory.

In fashioning this vessel of mine, God gifted me with the love of music. I've composed many songs and poems over the years that I would someday like to publish. One year, I recorded a soundtrack of ten songs at a recording studio and marketed them. As God opened doors for a singing ministry, I began ministering in song at Christian venues. Singing songs of hope and joy to the hurting and the lost filled my heart to overflowing.

MY BROKEN PIECES—HIS YIELDED CLAY

One of the songs I recorded reflected my life's journey as if the songwriter had written it just for me. Its lyrics summed up the deepest aspects of my valleys and mountaintop experiences. I thank God for bringing it into my life. I'd like to share some of the words from that song with you.

He Didn't Throw the Clay Away

Empty and broken, I came back to Him
A vessel unworthy, so scarred with sin
But He did not despair, He started over again
And I bless the day He didn't throw the clay away

Over and over, He molds me and makes me
Into His vessel, He fashions the clay
A vessel of honor I am today
All because Jesus didn't throw the clay away

He is the Potter, and I am the clay
Molded into His image, He wants me to stay
But when I stumble, and I fall
And my vessel breaks
Well He just picks up the pieces
He doesn't throw the clay away

A vessel of honor
I am today
All because Jesus didn't throw the clay away

I pray these lyrics are a source of encouragement for you as well. And I hope they point you to Jesus, the Potter who loves you, His cherished vessel of clay.

This part of my journey has come to fruition. It's time to pass on what God has done in my life and given me to share with others. It's all in His perfect timing, all a part of His perfect plan. Until God takes me home to be with Him for eternity, I want to serve Him to encourage, to give hope, to teach, and to bless others with the love of God through Christ who lives in my heart. Most importantly, I want to lift up the name of Jesus, glorify His name. I want to give Him praise, give Him honor, point souls to the cross, to Jesus, the author and perfecter of our faith.

Because of His finished work on the cross, we can now proclaim to the world that He is our Savior and Redeemer, the One who died in our place for the forgiveness of sins. He was nailed to the cross so that we might have life more abundantly and free. And through His shed blood for the redemption of our sins, we can now be saved by His grace. We don't have to earn our salvation; it's a gift from Jesus to all who seek Him.

I don't know what tomorrow holds. But I know *who* holds my hand. To God be the glory for the things He has done in my life, has brought me through, and has yet to do. There is hope in the name of the Lord. Believe it. Trust in Him. He can take all your broken pieces and put them back together again. Be that "yielded vessel."

The end is just the beginning. Hallelujah and amen!

Love, Evie

ABOUT THE AUTHOR

Evie G. is a happily retired elementary school teacher who has had a passion for writing since she was a child. She continually creates poems and songs that reflect her profound love of the Lord. As a Christian, the love of music led her to becoming a worship leader and to recording an album of Christian songs. She teaches healing and restoration classes for women at her church, sings in the choir, and involves herself with serving the Lord wherever He leads. The loves of her life are her two children, four grandchildren, and six great-grandchildren. In her spare time, she enjoys planting a garden every year and digging in the soil with her grandchildren. Her hobbies are crafting of all kinds and making benches out of repurposed headboards and footboards. One of her greatest joys is making tortillas with her family, and baking with her grandchildren. She lives in a small town named Winton, in Central California, where she is surrounded by those she loves and thanks God for the gift of life each day.

CPSIA information can be obtained
at www.ICGtesting.com
Printed in the USA
LVHW101157190423
744759LV00001B/5